THE MUSES OF GWINN

THE LIBRARY of

AMERICAN
LANDSCAPE
HISTORY

THE MUSES OF GWINN

Art and Nature in
a Garden Designed by
Warren H. Manning
Charles A. Platt
& Ellen Biddle Shipman

ROBIN KARSON

SAGAPRESS, INC.

In Association With
THE LIBRARY OF
AMERICAN LANDSCAPE HISTORY, INC.

Distributed By
HARRY N. ABRAMS, INC.

The Library of American Landscape History, a not-for-profit corporation, was founded in the belief that clear, informative books about American landscape design will broaden support for enlightened preservation. Library publications are intended for landscape historians, members of the profession and the interested public. *The Muses of Gwinn* is the inaugural volume in the Designers and Places series.

The board of directors thanks the LALH editorial advisors, Keith N. Morgan, Boston University; Catha Grace Rambusch, Wave Hill; David C. Streatfield, University of Washington; William H. Tishler, University of Wisconsin-Madison; and Suzanne L. Turner, Louisiana State University. We are particularly grateful for the generous research and production subsidies that have helped bring this book to print.

Nancy R. Turner, President; John Franklin Miller, Clerk; Michael Karson, Treasurer; Eleanor G. Ames and Nesta Spink.

Photographs of Gwinn on pages ii, iii, vi, viii, 2, 40, 94, 95, 96, 98, 105, 138, and jacket front copyright © 1995 by Carol Betsch
Edited by Carol Betsch
Design and composition by Sandra Mattielli, Laura Shaw and Greg Endries
Production coordinated by Carol Lewis
Printed in Hong Kong

Library of Congress Cataloging-in-Publication Data

Karson, Robin S.
    The Muses of Gwinn : art and nature in a garden designed by Warren H. Manning, Charles A. Platt & Ellen Biddle Shipman / Robin Karson.
        p.   cm.
    "In association with the Library of American Landscape History."
    Includes bibliographical references (p. 187) and index.
    ISBN 0-89831-034-2 (Sagapress) / ISBN 0-8109-4292-5 (Abrams)
    1. Gwinn Estate Gardens (Cleveland, Ohio) 2. Mather, William Gwinn, 1851-1951—Homes and Haunts—Ohio. 3. Manning, Warren H. (Warren Henry), 1860-1938, 4. Platt, Charles A. (Charles Adams), 1861-1933, 5. Shipman, Ellen. I. Mather, William Gwinn, 1857-1951. II. Library of American Landscape History. III. Title.
SB466.U7G884   1995
712' .6' 097732—dc20   95-8157

For my mother
and father

An exhibition entitled
"Gwinn: A Portrait of the Garden,"
which includes photographs from this book,
has been organized by
the Library of American Landscape History for
the Cleveland Botanical Garden.

CONTENTS

PREFACE

Three years ago, I put aside a survey I was writing about the landscapes of the Country Place Era and turned instead to a shorter, more detailed study of one particularly fine example of the period. Gwinn, circa 1907, located in an eastern suburb of Cleveland, Ohio, seemed worthy of extended research for several reasons. Because three important designers—Charles Platt, Warren Manning, and Ellen Shipman—had worked there, a study of the estate presented an exceptional opportunity to compare different landscape approaches. The survival of a near-complete set of letters written during Gwinn's development furnished a window onto this unusual collaboration. The Gwinn correspondence seemed particularly valuable as few complete sets of letters related to any job by Platt, Manning, or Shipman have survived.

Additionally, Gwinn's date positioned it near the beginning of an interesting and important period in American landscape history. Because Gwinn was featured repeatedly in the contemporary literature, it was influential in the general development of the American country house and landscape movement. Finally, because Gwinn was, in many respects, both a typical and a "landmark" work, a careful study of it seemed likely to reveal many of the period's design principles. One important theme—tension between formal and informal elements—was central to Gwinn's design.

It is ironic that the future of most country place landscapes—nearly all of which were commissioned by wealthy and eminently private Americans—now depends on their making a transition to public use. Gwinn underwent this change four decades ago, earlier and more gracefully than many landscapes of its kind. The foresight of Gwinn's first stewards, William Gwinn and Elizabeth Ring Mather, and the extensive restorations undertaken by their successors, Cornelia and James Ireland, set an unusually energetic preservation standard.

The estate's current executive director, Lucy Ireland Weller, faces new challenges as architecture, furnishings, and plants continue to age.

When I discovered the archival resources at Gwinn, I proposed a research project that might offer help to the estate's staff. They agreed that a monograph exploring Gwinn's social, artistic, and historic contexts would aid them as they pursued day-to-day maintenance and planned for the estate's future. The resulting volume, one of the first collaborations between Sagapress and the Library of American Landscape History, is published with the hope that it will enhance not only Gwinn's future but, by example, the future of other cultural landscapes in the United States.

Part One of this book provides the background context against which the particulars of Gwinn's story can be better understood. Since little has been published about any of the principal characters involved (with the exception of Keith N. Morgan's Platt monograph, which focuses on architecture rather than landscape architecture), lengthy biographical sketches were written to accompany the discussion of aesthetic and cultural perspectives on the period's landscapes. Part Two presents a chronological narrative of the actual development and implementation of Gwinn's design. It is hoped that general and professional audiences will find both sections of interest. Endnotes offer citation sources and more detailed information for the specialist. Quotations have not been edited to current botanical convention.

All archival photographs, unless otherwise noted, are from the William Gwinn Mather Papers, Gwinn Archives, Gwinn Estate, Cleveland, Ohio. Facsimile reproductions are by William Baltz, of Cleveland, Ohio.

ROBIN KARSON

PART ONE

BACKGROUND

The fountain terrace, 1993. Photograph by Carol Betsch

CHAPTER ONE

INTRODUCTION TO GWINN

IN 1907 CHARLES A. PLATT and Warren H. Manning—both pivotal figures in the history of American landscape architecture—found themselves working together on the shores of Lake Erie. They were hired by a Cleveland industrialist, William Gwinn Mather, to collaborate on the design of a new house and landscape in the eastern suburbs. The twenty-seven-acre estate that resulted from their labors figures among the finest examples of American landscape architecture of the period.

The collaborative arrangement may have exaggerated the differences between Gwinn's designers' aesthetic approaches. At the very least, it located the design process in a series of dialogues. These exchanges, most of which were recorded in letters, spanned more than a quarter century. The aesthetic tension between Platt and Manning appears to have inspired both men: Gwinn figures among the best landscapes designed by either of them.

Two women also played important though limited roles in Gwinn's development. Ellen Biddle Shipman worked at Gwinn first in 1914 and on several occasions during the 1930s and 1940s.[1] Her planting plans for the estate's formal garden filled the architectural framework established by Platt in the first phase of the project. Elizabeth Ring Mather, William's wife, moved to Gwinn in 1929, long after most of the broad landscape decisions had been made. Her subtle influence on later developments is surely pervasive, but we can most clearly see Elizabeth's ideas in the planting designs for the formal garden developed with Ellen Shipman in the 1930s.

One other woman, Katharine Mather, William's older half-sister who lived at Gwinn from 1908 until William married in 1929, probably was also influential in the estate's design, but letters to Manning, Platt, and Shipman bear William's (and later, Elizabeth's) signature only and rarely refer to his sister's ideas. Although it would be satisfying to bring Kate's ideas to life, we simply do not have the evidence to do so.

Many contemporary journals and books featured Gwinn—even *National Geographic* ran a photograph and caption in a 1932 piece about Ohio.[2] It is interesting that the estate was often identified as an original *American* work, despite the architecture's obvious Italian borrowings. Stylish and photogenic, Platt's structural framework and Manning's lush plantings influenced designers and homeowners across the country.

In 1909, just months after the house was completed, the *Architectural Record* published a rapturous account of Gwinn in an issue devoted to new phases in American domestic architecture. The design was applauded as "an admirable example of the successful and spirited carrying out of one dominant idea"—a celebration of the lake—and contrasted with eclectic designs that borrowed motifs from widely disparate traditions and periods.[3] Other glowing accounts of Gwinn followed rapidly. In 1912 *National Architect*, *American Country Houses of To-day*, *Architecture*, and *Country Life in America* all published descriptions and photographs of the estate.[4] The following year Platt's office issued a monograph of his work with an introduction by Royal Cortissoz. The book featured eighteen pages of photographs of Gwinn, inside and out. "[Platt] is all taste, and his work, from beginning to end, has been remarkable for its fitness and restraint," wrote Cortissoz. The author emphasized Platt's originality and his responsivity to site: "The old Italian ideal is so tactfully and with such sincerity adjusted to local conditions that the completed work becomes part and parcel of a veritable characteristic American home."[5]

In 1915 Louis Shelton, author of *Beautiful Gardens in America*, identified Gwinn's garden as "undoubtedly the most notable in the state." That same year, Samuel Howe included it in *American Country Houses of To-day*.[6] The undated *Studies in Landscape Architecture*, edited by a committee of the Boston Society of Landscape Architects, featured a photograph of Gwinn's entry drive as an example of Warren Manning's work. A. D. Taylor used an image of Gwinn's pergola for the frontispiece of his 1929 book, *The Complete Garden*. Gwinn was also featured in a 1934 article in *Your Garden and Home* and in Fitch and Rockwell's *Treasury of American Gardens* in 1956.[7]

One of the longest articles about Gwinn appeared in May 1916 in the popular British magazine *Country Life*.[8] There the estate was praised as "a many-sided, many-coloured place, varying in its texture, full of an aesthetic magnetism." (*Town and Country* had used the very same phrase in their article the previous year.)[9] The writer, Samuel Howe, was especially enthusiastic about Gwinn's "straightforward, wholesome and distinguished manner—a manner as direct as it is unaffected." He contrasted Gwinn with heavy-handed copies of European designs, finding it "refreshing to the average citizen who has become tired of the tyranny of style, who is wearied of timid approaches to architectural problems, wearied, too, of the domination of materials and of fantastic methods of representing old traditions."

Howe also appreciated the grandeur of the lake view: "The idea of so contriving a property as to embrace the lake, with its silvery grey mist and its reverberations of a fantastic melody, has seemed beyond the dreams of the imagination. Think of having a lake of your own a hundred miles long, the boundaries of which no eye can determine, and to know that it is yours for ever, and that it cannot be taken from you."

CHAPTER TWO

FORMAL AND INFORMAL DESIGN IN THE COUNTRY PLACE ERA

GWINN OFFERS an especially rich case study for the student of aesthetics since it embodies a debate between formal and informal landscape principles, one of the key theoretical arguments of the period. Charles Platt, a formalist, was the architect of record for the house and landscape architect for site planning on the five-acre home grounds. Warren Manning, an advocate of informality, designed planting plans for Gwinn's home grounds in 1908 and, beginning in 1914, circulation, structures, and plantings for the twenty-one-acre wild garden across Lake Shore Boulevard. Mather hired Manning in 1906 and Platt in 1907 and negotiated their often conflicting recommendations for the next quarter century. He could scarcely have opted for two more contrasting aesthetic orientations, yet both seemed to inspire him. He was not alone in the polarity of his tastes.

Contemporary popular and professional journals traced the same conflict in print. The tension was cast as a choice between formality and informality, the architectonic and the naturalistic, and "European" versus "American" style. At one end of the continuum were geometrically determined landscapes that took their cues from the house and were structured by architectural elements; at the other extreme were landscapes of rolling lawns, meadows, shrubberies, and woodlands where the civilizing hand of the gardener was almost invisible. The American debate was presaged in Britain by the animated conflict between William Robinson, proponent of the wild garden, and Reginald Blomfield, advocate of formalism.[1] While the American version was conducted in less heated tones, it represented no less profound an ideological clash. For the most part, the new American elite wanted dignified and culturally meaningful homes and gardens; at the same time, many of them longed for vital, "natural," even rustic incidents specifically because such elements were interpreted as indigenous.

The argument between formalists and proponents of American naturalism did not focus solely or even primarily on questions of aesthetics. Style had deeper social, cultural, and even political reverberations. Some new clients were drawn to the democratic spirit of a woodland outlook, others sought the patrician elegance of a portico. Formal and informal landscape features not only expressed different values, they also led to different experiences of nature. Woods, meadows, and fields imparted a sense of connection to the natural world, pergolas and teahouses precipitated the opposite feeling: nature as a spectacle to be appreciated from a distance, a phenomenon apart. Both sides had their advocates, but the fountain's splash—with its evocation of privilege, exclusion, and dominion over nature—was a comforting sound to many new homeowners, including William Mather.

One of the first writers to address the dilemma of style during the period was Mrs. (Mariana) Schuyler Van Rensselaer. Her influential book of 1893, *Art Out-of-Doors*, urged readers to avoid the dichotomy that pitted formal and naturalistic gardening against one another as "deadly rivals, each of which must put the knife to the other's throat if it wishes itself to survive."[2] In Van Rensselaer's view "the only right theory is that no theory is always right—that good sense and good taste must dictate the specially appropriate solution for each special problem." The author, however, did encourage greater familiarity with the formal style for most Americans, who, in her opinion, tended to overlook it in designing small town gardens where naturalism inevitably backfired. But she also professed the view that "naturalistic methods of gardening are the most interesting and important to Americans," and advocated the use of "local" plants. J. Horace McFarland, Warren Manning's influential colleague and cofounder of the American Park and Outdoor Art Association, took Van Rensselaer's recommendations a step further and proposed an American landscape style based exclusively on native plants. McFarland's 1899 article "An American Garden" featured a rhapsodic description of one of Manning's early wild gardens, Dolobran.[3] McFarland championed Manning's creation as a prime example of a "distinctively American" landscape, praising the "free beauty of native woodland, marsh, and copse." He contrasted this approach with "that extreme cultivated barbarism called 'Italian gardening,' with its clipped and sheared yews and box trees." In poetic prose, McFarland extolled both the use of American plants and what he identified as an American *style* of growing plants: free and open—in his word, "democratic."

The debate continued. In 1902 it was addressed head-on in an *Architectural Record* article titled "The Formal and the Natural Style."[4] The author, an architect, interpreted the formal garden revival as a reaction to "the over-appreciative enthusiasm" for "the romantic or natural style." Like Van Rensselaer, he argued that each school was "capable of producing works of extraordinary beauty" and begged his professional readers to be flexible in their orientation. He argued that "the constant tendency of those with predilections for the natural school . . . to overlook [the] fundamental question of fitness" had caused landscape architects to lose many jobs to architects. The fact that the two professions were often competing for the same work undoubtedly led to mounting tension between the disciplines and may have served to polarize approaches.

The search for a naturalistic American style was advanced most energetically by Wilhelm Miller, an editor for *Country Life in America*. "Let every country use chiefly its own native trees, shrubs, and vines and other permanent material," Miller wrote in 1911, "and let the style of gardening grow naturally out of necessity, the soil and the new conditions. When we stop imitating and do this, America will soon find herself." Miller identified the new style, inspired by midwestern plains landscapes, as the "prairie spirit in landscape gardening."[5]

His writing championed in particular the work of the outspoken and charismatic Jens Jensen, a Danish immigrant who had gotten his start working for the Chicago Parks Department. During a long and successful career, Jensen designed private estates for Henry and son Edsel Ford, and many others equally prominent, as well as several large parks in and around Chicago. Increasingly, Jensen's designs, public and private, featured native plant palettes and sinuous spaces that flowed as they might in nature. An influential conservationist, writer, and inspired polemicist, Jensen opened the 1926 meeting of the American Society of Landscape Architects with the warning that formal gardens were "inappropriate to the manner of life of our people." According to Robert E. Grese, Jensen's biographer, "the relative merits of formal versus informal design and of native versus non-native plants were [then] debated, but a consensus was not reached."[6]

Although Jensen and his midwestern colleagues tended to merge the use of native plants with an informal stylistic approach, many practitioners did not. Charles Platt, for example, often used native plants in his highly architectural schemes; other naturalistically oriented designers, including Olmsted Sr., used exotics even in their wild gardens. Warren Manning was among those who did not believe that imported plants must, by definition, be rigorously avoided in the new American garden. He frequently relied on native plants because they were inexpensive, readily available, easy to transplant, and, in most cases, easy to grow, but he used exotic species, too, focusing on their design effect, not their geographic pedigree.[7]

The basis of the informal approach to landscape design in America can be traced to the works and writings of Andrew Jackson Downing, who looked to Walpole's England for his inspiration. But it is no surprise that the American formal garden movement stemmed from the architectural developments of the period. McKim, Mead and White, Carrère and Hastings, Delano and Aldrich, William Welles Bosworth, Charles Platt, and dozens of other architects routinely designed landscapes in conjunction with residences according to Beaux-Arts principles of spatial layout and ornament. These architects tended to approach the landscape as though it were an extension of the house, and defined it largely through architectural means. In general, their designs responded only minimally to the pre-existing conditions of the site. Many consulted with landscape architects about planting.

One architect who did his own planting design and achieved considerable prominence in the gardening world was Guy Lowell. Lowell's widely read survey, *American Gardens*, published in 1902, featured formal gardens almost without exception.[8] But Lowell's heavily ornamented schemes and those of many of his architectural colleagues lacked real horticultural feeling. Photographs testify to their hard-edged, almost bombastic deliberateness.

Charles Platt's more secure Italian formality was grounded in the (then) revolutionary concept of use: "It is essential," he wrote, "that 'the punishment fit the crime'; that the house be suited to the family that will live in it." To Platt's way of thinking, both the architecture and the landscape would "grow logically out of the life to be lived in the new house."[9]

Platt's vision was nurtured in the fervid atmosphere of the artists' colony in Cornish, New Hampshire, where the American Renaissance movement flourished. The movement was based on the idea that a new, American style could be built on classical prototypes; in this sense, it represented the opposite of Miller's and Jensen's view, which emphasized the importance of native plants and landscape forms as stylistic motifs. In Platt's designs, the classical, largely Italian, impulse combined with an Arts and Crafts appreciation of materials and workmanship to provide a new, formal prototype for American gardens. Platt was hailed by many critics, including his fellow Cornishite Herbert Croly, as the progenitor of the longed-for modern American style.[10]

The American debate over naturalism and formalism continued through the second and third decades of the new century. During the period, a compromise evolved that judiciously balanced the two; in the words of one writer, "some measure of formality, combined with a thoroughly informal scheme of planting."[11] According to a widely accepted approach that had its roots in England, formal elements were recommended for development near and in relation to the house; increasingly naturalistic schemes could then unfold toward the perimeter of the designed landscape. This approach characterized the work of the country's largest firm, Olmsted Brothers, except in rare cases when stylistic flexibility was needed for business reasons, for example, when the client wanted something different.

In the final analysis, few of the period's landscape architects were absolute purists: Manning's designs, many of which were conceived in collaboration with architects, usually included terraces and straight walks; Platt's designs, many of which were conceived in collaboration with landscape architects, often included areas of informal planting. At Gwinn, where the two points of view jostled for dominance, the tension spawned an unusual vitality.

While an unprecedented combination of factors created a large market for residences like Gwinn, the most significant new development was economic: from 1890 until the stock market crashed in 1929, more people made more money than ever before. "By 1910," reports Mark Hewitt in *The Architect and the American Country House*, "there were 15,090 families with incomes of more than $50,000—an amount defining an urban-industrial upper class capable of having country houses." (Such an income, Hewitt points out, would have allowed $100,000 worth of house and land and an operating budget of $7,500.)[12]

Land was plentiful, construction costs relatively low, and an influx of European immigrants trained in the domestic arts began to arrive just in time to service the large houses and make the gardens grow. Several university programs for landscape architects were established during the century's early years and attracted scores of talented, artistic men and women. A professional organization, the American Society of Landscape Architects (ASLA), was founded in 1899—by Warren Manning and ten of his colleagues—to set standards of ethics and practice. Literally thousands of grand-scale residential landscapes were created during the period. Biltmore, in Asheville, North Carolina, generally considered the era's first country place, was also its largest with 255 rooms and eventually 125,000 acres; many, like Gwinn (which had only 16 rooms and covered about 27 acres), were considerably less palatial but more successful in purely aesthetic terms.

The growing ranks of early twentieth-century American landscape designers were heirs to a distinguished body of knowledge and work. Through his writings and far-ranging practice, Frederick Law Olmsted Sr. was instrumental in defining the profession in the United States. Because his landscape legacy was carefully studied by his immediate successors, Biltmore, Olmsted's last project, acquired special significance. The estate's design announced many of the themes that would shape large-scale residential work over the next four decades, but more important, it set an example: Olmsted's students could scarcely fail to observe that the country's most famous landscape architect accepted a commission for a country house landscape at the end of his career.

The term "Country Place Era" captures one important aspect of the period's residential landscapes: they were designed to bring the lives of their owners into closer contact with the outdoors.[13] But while clients often referred to their new homes as "country places," many estates, including Gwinn, were not really in the country at all but on the outskirts of large cities. Rail and electric streetcar systems were facilitating commuting just as the steady deterioration of urban conditions made flight from the city increasingly appealing. From Long Island to Santa Barbara, Mount Desert Island to Sarasota, country houses sprang up wherever new wealth accumulated and residents could find a breeze and a view.

The demand for country houses far exceeded the availability of old ones on the market, but the American building boom was also precipitated by changing tastes. The dark, irregular interiors of Victorian homes began to seem provincial as legions of wealthy Americans traveled abroad and visited country houses with light-filled interiors and expansive pleasure grounds. They also read about European country houses in dozens of new home and landscape periodicals (*Country Life in America*, for example), which coached anxious subscribers in every conceivable aspect of the new life style, including leisure pursuits, fashion, food, and, of course, gardens.

For many American clients, a new country house—like the ones they visited in France, England, or Italy—held the promise of instant cultural and social status. As a result, architects and landscape architects were often asked to incorporate clearly identifiable European architectural models into their designs, almost as souvenirs from their clients' travels. During the 1920s, American gardens became increasingly exotic, functioning almost as stage sets for the carefully plotted social lives of their owners. These scrapbook approaches, however, often lacked the vital input of the clients' real backgrounds and interests.

Unlike some art forms, architecture and landscape architecture depended on patrons, not all of whom proved ideal artistic partners. "The ordinary American," wrote Herbert Croly in 1909,

> conceived the architect as a sort of a broker, whose business it was to carry out his ideas. He usually bought his site and decided on the location of his house without taking any expert advice. He deemed himself quite competent to decide what kind of a house the site demanded, how it should be approached, in what direction it should face, what trees should be chopped down and where new ones should be planted.... If he was a very rich man he probably wanted a much bigger and more ostentatious house than was warranted by the site. If he was a traveled man he may have brought home from the other side the vision of some Italian palace or Jacobean manor house, which he must have, no matter how little they were suited to the surroundings."[14]

More valuable, from an aesthetic perspective, were those rarer clients, such as William Mather, who brought taste, restraint, and respect for professional training to the process.

Although clients naturally sought compatible personalities when choosing their designers, landscape projects often profited from a certain lack of harmony. Challenges presented by personal and site-specific idiosyncrasies could make designers stretch beyond conventional solutions. At Gwinn, the design process was unusually complex, as three strong personalities each had their say. Although Gwinn was certainly not the period's only project in which creative aesthetic solutions were hammered out after long argument, it remains one of the few in which we can confidently untangle the differing points of view.

Charles A. Platt, 1923. Photograph by Pirie MacDonald.
Courtesy, members of the Platt family

The Muses of Gwinn

CHAPTER THREE

CHARLES A. PLATT, WARREN H. MANNING, AND ELLEN BIDDLE SHIPMAN

BORN TO PARENTS of ample means and strong cultural interests, Charles Adams Platt (1861–1933) enjoyed a happy childhood in New York City. By his own report, his formal education included "neither long nor thorough" art training at the Art Students League and the National Academy of Design.[1] After a chance meeting with Stephen Parrish (father of the painter Maxfield Parrish), Platt became his pupil, studying the newly revived art of etching. Platt's sure eye and ability to simplify multiple elements into strong compositions led him to sudden critical success. Yet he did not consider etching the ideal vehicle to fully express his talents. At age twenty-one, Platt moved to Paris to become a painter.

When all of his canvases were rejected by the Salon of 1883, and those that were accepted the following year were ignored by the exhibition catalogue, Platt decided to enroll in the Académie Julian to pursue instruction. His fellow students in the informal atelier included Will Low, Kenyon Cox, and Willard Metcalf.[2] Platt continued to paint but also became interested in architecture. Although he was unsuccessful in his application to the architectural section of the Ecole des Beaux-Arts, Platt later credited his preparation for the entrance examination with introducing him to the basic principles of the art.[3]

While studying in Paris, Platt fell in love with an American woman, Annie Hoe, whom he married in Italy in 1886. Their union was short-lived and tragic, however; in 1887 Annie died in childbirth along with the Platts' newborn twin girls. Devastated, Charles returned alone to New York.

Platt's reaction to this tragedy may have strengthened an aesthetic stance that had already emerged in his painting—specifically, a preference for the "beautiful" over the "picturesque," in Keith Morgan's words, "a rejection of the curious, decayed, and irregular."[4] Platt's deliberate shunning of realism in art may have reflected a desire to avoid it in life, where the vagaries of fate had brought him excruciating losses. For whatever reason, he would continue to seek balance, harmony, and perfect classical form in all his art.

In 1889 Platt joined his friend Henry Oliver Walker for several weeks of sketching in Cornish, New Hampshire, where a colony of artists and writers had gathered around the sculptor Augustus Saint-Gaudens. Life in Cornish offered a robust combination of work and play that included not only art but serious gardening and garden making.[5] "One night when a number of us were dining with Maxfield Parrish," wrote Ellen Shipman (also a Cornish resident), "the talk had been so continually upon plants and diseases that he arose, put his hands on the table, and . . . said in a deep voice, 'Let us spray.'"[6]

Cornish summers included hard work during the day (visits before four in the afternoon were discouraged) and enthusiastic socializing in the evenings and on weekends. Colony residents enjoyed the lively pleasures of dining, sports, charades, masques, tableaux vivants, and the natural beauty of the Connecticut River Valley. The spirit of the American Renaissance movement was pervasive. Artists in all media looked to the example of the classical past for inspiration in their work; they also looked for opportunities to cross-pollinate disciplines. The beautiful physical setting, the general feeling of economic well-being, and the exciting notion that the United States was on the cusp of a new creative age offered a stimulating and harmonious context for making art.

The roster of the colony's resident luminaries included painters (both Stephen and Maxfield Parrish, George de Forest Brush, Kenyon Cox, Thomas Dewing, Everett Shinn, and Julian Alden Weir), writers (Herbert Croly, Winston Churchill, Rose Standish Nichols, Robert Herrick, and Maud Howe Elliot), sculptors

(Augustus Saint-Gaudens, Daniel Chester French, Herbert Adams, Paul Manship, Helen Mears), and Ellen Biddle Shipman and her husband, Louis Shipman, a playwright. Lesser-known composers, dancers, naturalists, publishers, singers, musicians, and designers also summered in Cornish. So did Ethel Barrymore and Ellen and Woodrow Wilson.

Cornish not only set the stage for Platt's architectural approach, it provided an incubator for the American country house movement generally. Platt, Augustus Saint-Gaudens, Maxfield Parrish, Daniel Chester French, and Julian Alden Weir—none of whom were trained architects—all contributed to the design of influential country houses and gardens during the colony's early years.

In 1890 Platt bought a piece of land not far from Saint-Gaudens's and began to design a house for it. He sited the simple clapboard residence in the rolling hills to overlook sheep pastures and a distant view of the Connecticut River. Platt's sensitivity to the larger picture and his interest in creating visual and psychological connections between the house and the garden were evident even at this early stage. His trip to Italy in 1886 had given him a firsthand look at villa gardens. After a return trip in 1892, he would successfully apply several Italian principles to the development of his own garden. Platt's friends and artistic colleagues encouraged him in his early pursuit of architecture by offering interest, advice, and, in a few cases, paying jobs.

Platt's first professional commission came from his neighbor in Cornish, Annie Lazarus, who owned the crest of a barren hill opposite his. The site called for a different approach from the one he had taken with his own residence, which despite certain Italianate aspects more resembled a New England farmhouse than a Tuscan villa. For Lazrus's High Court, Platt may have consciously decided to follow the lead of the architectural firm of McKim, Mead and White, who were also looking at Italian prototypes for inspiration. While working on the commission, the young architect ingenuously asked the more experienced Stanford White, with whom he was friendly, for "some photos or something that would help me in regard to detail."[7]

High Court won widespread admiration, especially for its garden. Ellen Shipman later wrote: "The valley was still filled with rolling clouds...the moon was full and had risen above them. In the distance was Ascutney Mountain,... and just a few feet below where we stood upon a terrace, was a Sunken Garden with rows bathed in moonlight of white lilies standing as an altar for Ascutney."[8]

Platt's second trip to Italy in 1892 was undertaken, in part, to introduce his brother William, a young landscape architect, to the beauties of formal design.

William's mentor, Olmsted Sr., did not approve of the tour. "I am afraid that I do not think much of the fine and costly gardening of Italy," he warned, recommending instead the "roadside foreground scenery." Olmsted's fundamental aesthetic view—the virtual opposite of Charles Platt's—was captured in his closing: "I urge you again to hunt for beauty in commonplace and pleasant conditions."[9] Nevertheless, the brothers went ahead with their plans; the Villa d'Este, the Villa Farnese, and the Villa Lante were among several they visited and photographed.

Less than a month after returning from Italy, Charles's brother drowned while vacationing in Portland, Maine. Grief-stricken, the artist again buried himself in his work. Platt's Cornish garden, considerably expanded according to Italian examples he had recently seen, was one of the projects that distracted him. Another was a relationship with Eleanor Bunker, widow of his friend Dennis Bunker. Eleanor was beautiful, talented, and, like Platt, recovering from the loss of a spouse. They married in 1893.

The union seemed to give energy and focus to Platt's vocational efforts. He submitted two illustrated articles about the 1892 Italian trip to *Harper's Magazine* and signed a contract with Harper and Brothers for a book on the subject. *Italian Gardens*, published in 1894, featured Platt's handsome, brooding photographs and a short narrative text. The text drew criticism from within the profession—Charles Eliot, who had joined the Olmsted firm as a full partner the previous year, thought it "unsatisfactory" in its lack of scholarship—but the heavily illustrated volume was popular with the public and catalyzed interest in the Italian style.[10] Platt's book was followed a decade later by Edith Wharton's influential *Italian Villas and Their Gardens*, illustrated by Maxfield Parrish.[11]

Italian Gardens brought Platt into the public eye, earning him his first commission outside Cornish. Dr. and Mrs. John Elliot hired him in 1895 to design their new house and garden in Needham, Massachusetts. He also quickly landed more local commissions. One of these, for his friend Herbert Croly, the editor of the *Architectural Record*, was among the projects Mather reviewed during his search for an architect for Gwinn.

Two early landscape designs made Platt's national reputation. He began Faulkner Farm in 1897 and Weld in 1901.[12] Both were located in Brookline, Massachusetts, just a few miles apart and, coincidentally, near the headquarters of the expanding Olmsted firm. Critics recognized Platt's designs as reworkings of Italian Renaissance prototypes but nevertheless hailed their new American qualities. The well-known architect Ralph Adams Cram observed: "Conceived on thoroughly modern and original lines, [Platt's designs] make no pretense at deceiving one into thinking he has been suddenly transferred to some unfamiliar Italian villa."[13] Both projects were published widely and left strong visual impressions on legions of prospective clients.

As his practice and stature grew, Platt came to insist on designing both house and garden, because he felt, in the Italian tradition, that the indoor-outdoor relationship was critically important. His ability to conceptualize an estate as a single design idea and to adapt the design to meet the real day-to-day needs of his clients distinguished him among his colleagues. Although he was not the only, or the first, architect who treated the house and garden as a single design unit, he quickly became the most prominent.[14] During his most productive years—the 1890s until World War I, when the estate market shrank dramatically—Platt created some of the country's most artistically satisfying country houses.

In 1904 Platt took the opportunity to disparage the nineteenth-century Victorian residence as "the dime novel of architecture." This he caricatured as "a much-begabled house, prodigal in lattices and window seats, charged upon by a riot of flower beds, and surrounded by nooks and walks." In its place, Platt recommended a "roomy house, built upon models of good tradition, not aggressively beamed or wainscotted or latticed into originality, but having a sense of style . . . as restful as the lines of its suitable and elegant garden."[15] Such houses, Platt recommended, should be "domesticated" from Italian and English examples—the latter, in his opinion, offered excellent models of Italian villas which had been adapted for year-round use. Without directly confronting his aesthetic opponents' point of view, Platt wrote that his clients scarcely wanted "to return to a state of nature"; in his experience, even in the country, they would continue to "read, dine, entertain, dress, and have leisure much as in town."

Platt's formulaic approach to landscape design served him well. Nearly all his country house estates included a formal approach and courtyard, a service approach and service courtyard, and areas of relative informality including vistas and panoramas, groves of usually indigenous trees, and wide sweeps of lawn, all of which provided foils for architecturally determined spaces. Garages, gardeners' and caretakers' cottages, garden walls, gates, and service areas were also usually included, as widespread period practices dictated. However, Platt's sense of proportion, his ability to see the plan as a whole, and his capacity to anticipate the visual impact of one area on another were extraordinary.

Platt's formal gardens varied in size and elaboration in accordance with the size and importance of the house. Nearly always bilaterally symmetrical and laid out in axial relation to the house, they usually included a central greensward or pool surrounded and defined by gravel footpaths; clipped bay trees that marked intersecting paths; pergolas, pavilions, teahouses, and other diminutive architectural structures at the long ends of the major garden spaces; water features, including pools and fountains, as focal points; and box hedges bordering exuberant flower beds. Urns, columns, planters, sarcophagi, well curbs, benches, wall fountains, herms, and other sculptural forms served as axial termini and accents. Connections between the house and garden were clearly articulated by sight lines and physical circulation.

Platt's planting approach was architectural: plants were objects—albeit living objects—in much the same sense as balustrades and columns. Although he possessed greater horticultural awareness than most of his architectural colleagues, his plant repertory was not large, nor his interest particularly keen. Platt's most successful landscapes, including Gwinn, were conceived and executed in collaboration with landscape architects.[16]

Platt was, by all accounts, a pleasant though initially chilly person who eventually revealed a charming and dry wit. Slight and of medium height, he sported a full head of brown hair, a flowing mustache, small beard, and "bushy eyebrows which he raised and lowered individually or together," his son, Geoffrey Platt, recalled. "This gesture was very effective in conveying his reaction to what had just been said or done, and was more expressive than words."[17] Despite his quiet demeanor, Platt was fiercely competitive and an avid participant in games of tennis, golf, bridge, and—a Cornish favorite—croquet. He spoke French fluently, Italian less so, played the piano, enjoyed opera, and toured Europe annually, mixing pleasure with the business of shopping for his clients. His second marriage was a lasting and successful partnership, eventually producing five children.

During the course of Platt's long practice, he completed about 250 projects, ranging from houses and gardens to schools, campuses, museums, and office buildings. One major client was the Astor Estate Office, for whom he designed commercial buildings, hotels, residences, apartments, and interiors.[18] Platt's most ambitious public work was for the University of Illinois, Urbana, and Phillips Academy in Andover, Massachusetts; for both institutions Platt designed campus plans and many individual buildings. His 1924 design for the National Gallery of Art in Washington, D.C., went unrealized when Congress failed to approve the necessary funding.

In 1912, as his design work at Gwinn was drawing to a close, Platt was the focus of an article in *Landscape Architecture*. (It is noteworthy that the official quarterly of the American Society of Landscape Architects featured a practitioner from outside the organization's ranks, particularly since a keen rivalry existed between the two professions. Platt was politically savvy; he joined the ASLA as a corresponding member the year after the article appeared.) Charles Downing Lay, a well-known landscape architect in his own right, praised Platt as one who had mastered, "as has hardly any other man of modern times," the domains of architecture *and* landscape architecture. When Lay asked Platt for his advice to members of the sister profession, Platt issued a warning against being bound too closely by the natural conditions of the site: "rather remould them nearer to the heart's desire."[19] As a basic aesthetic approach, it could scarcely have differed more from that of his design partner at Gwinn.

Warren Henry Manning (1860–1938) saw the foundations of his professional life as, quite literally, rooted in the mud. "My education was begun by my mother leading me about the home garden and showing me birds, flowers, toads, butterflies, and beetles," Manning wrote in his autobiography. "Seeing my first snake was a thrilling event.... I modelled in sand and mud hills, valleys, tunnels, houses, roads, and gardens with pools. The trees were branchy weed tops; there were moss lawns, and tiny weeds and other flowers for the garden." Manning identified his mother, Lydia, a watercolorist, as the primary inspiration for his interest in nature. He also credited her with instilling in him a lifelong devotion to "making America a finer place in which to live."[20]

Warren and his four brothers were often asked to help with the housework, to cook, and bake bread. It may have been these early experiences, and his close relationship with his mother, that gave Manning an unusually sympathetic bearing toward women. Over the course of his long practice, he hired fifty-three women as assistants, secretaries, and consultants, an astonishing number in comparison with the examples of his male contemporaries.[21]

Manning also greatly admired his father, Jacob Warren Manning, whose Reading, Massachusetts, nursery—one of the country's finest—was the site of young Warren's long horticultural apprenticeship. Manning credited his father with being the first to take cuttings from the Concord grape, introducing the Woodward arborvitae into culture (for which he won a medal from the Massachusetts Horticultural Society), and for discovering and promoting the use of many unusual ornamental plants and many improved varieties of fruits. "From his nursery," Manning later wrote, "plants went to nearly every state in the union and many foreign countries."[22]

By 1884 the younger Manning had begun to design landscapes for his father's customers; a pamphlet from that year advertises that his availability to "make sketches and lay out grounds."[23] Manning's autobiography records no formal

Warren Manning. Warren H. Manning Collection, Center for Lowell
History, University of Massachusetts at Lowell

design training, so he was probably largely self-taught. Manning, like Olmsted, was never a skilled draftsman, nor was he particularly interested in mastering the architectural aspects of landscape design. Ironically, it may have been his lack of involvement in what one of his protegés, Fletcher Steele, identified as "the artistic side," that freed him to think systemically.[24] Manning's ability to grasp landscapes, cities, and entire regions as working systems was well suited to the tasks of town and campus planning. His understanding of landscapes as botanical, social, and even psychological environments, however, did not necessarily lead to memorable designs. Manning's most artistically successful residential designs, including Gwinn, were executed in conjunction with talented architects. In this respect, Manning's skills offered an exact complement to

Charles Platt's. The collaboration orchestrated by William Mather was no lucky accident—nor was it entirely based on Mather's dualistic sympathies with formal and informal design.

Manning supplemented his education with Saturday study sessions at the Arnold Arboretum and plant-hunting expeditions in the White Mountains of New Hampshire. Manning and his father also traveled to see other nursery operations and landscapes, including that of Charles Downing, brother of Andrew Jackson Downing, in Newburgh, New York. Warren's four younger brothers all participated in their father's business and eventually made horticulture their profession, too. Like Charles Platt, Warren Manning had a younger brother named William, who also worked for a time in the Olmsted office; by strange coincidence, both Williams died very young.

In 1888, three years after marrying Nellie Hamblin Pratt, Manning decided to leave his father's organization, "convinced," he later wrote, that he "must find a place with the most eminent man in the landscape profession—Frederick Law Olmsted." Impressed with his strong horticultural credentials, Olmsted Sr. agreed to hire the young plantsman.[25] Manning and his wife moved to Brookline, Massachusetts, and began a family, which eventually included one son and two daughters.

Manning's horticultural talents quickly became apparent in the Olmsted office, and he was given increasing responsibilities, chiefly in planting design. During his first month on the job, Manning later recalled, he was asked "to prepare plans for about sixteen widely-scattered properties" and was assigned several assistants.[26] Manning's stature in the Olmsted office was reflected by his selection in 1890 as the designer of the Brattle Street property of Charles W. Eliot, president of Harvard University.[27]

Among Manning's talented colleagues in the Brookline office were Frederick Olmsted Jr., John Charles Olmsted, and one of the country's most brilliant young landscape architects, Charles Eliot, son of the Harvard president. Eliot's work on the Boston Metropolitan Park System gave Manning firsthand exposure to revolutionary planning methods, the field in which he would later make his most lasting contributions. Manning's involvement with overlay maps during this period was particularly important; he later developed ingenious uses for them in conjunction with his own "cell-based" techniques for collecting and recording data in which each individual piece of information was entered into an appropriate "cell" or category. Manning's 1901 design for the park system in Harrisburg, Pennsylvania, which relied heavily on these methods, established him as a park planner of national importance.[28]

When Henry Sargent Codman, an Olmsted associate, died during preparations for the opening of the World's Columbian Exposition in Chicago in 1893, Manning was asked to oversee the final installation of plants—over one million of them, representing 2,300 species. Later, Manning proudly recalled Liberty Hyde Bailey's comment that the "general landscape features of the Exposition exceeded in boldness, originality, and artistic merit anything heretofore attempted."[29] The exposition also established Beaux-Arts classicism as America's prevailing architectural idiom—thereby preventing, in the estimation of many critics, the development of an indigenous school of American architecture. But the exposition marked other cultural watersheds, not only by proclaiming "the rise to maturity of the United States," as the British historians Geoffrey Jellicoe and Susan Jellicoe observed, but by announcing "the first truly American appreciation of the economic value of the arts in society."[30] Landscape design, of course, was one of those arts.

The largest and most influential residential commission to come to the Olmsted office during Manning's tenure was Biltmore, in Asheville, North Carolina. Shortly after George and Edith Vanderbilt purchased the old farm that would form the core of the estate, Olmsted Sr. advised them to "broaden and protect the outlook" by increasing their land holdings; Warren Manning was one of the group of advisers who climbed to the top of Mount Pisgah to determine what new property should be acquired.[31]

Olmsted's plan for the 125,000-acre estate made masterful use of widely varying terrain; it included a lake, approach drive, many miles of roads, pleasure grounds, formal gardens, park, farm, forest, and a small village. Manning avidly observed Olmsted's sensitivity to the lay of the land as his mentor determined planting and grading throughout the plan. Biltmore's forest management program, developed by Gifford Pinchot, later the first director of the U.S. Division of Forestry, was also studied with great interest by the young designer. On horseback, Manning supervised planting and compiled long lists of species, since Olmsted had interested the Vanderbilts in forming a "collection of all the woody plants that were likely to be hardy there."[32] Later, Manning would convince many of his own clients to form similar collections.

At Biltmore, Manning learned the intricacies of site design, but he also absorbed the unwritten codes guiding interactions between landscape architects, architects, and clients. Manning vividly remembered a confrontation between Olmsted and the Vanderbilts' architect, Richard Morris Hunt. One day while reviewing house plans, Olmsted criticized Hunt's design for its lack of a large terrace "from which the outlook can be enjoyed." According to Manning, Hunt tersely responded that such a feature would "not be in keeping with this type of house." Olmsted replied: "Then you have made an error in your selection of the house type."

"Mr. Vanderbilt," Manning continued, "watched his two designers with amusement in his eyes, without interjecting a word." In the end, Olmsted triumphed: "an open terrace at the southerly end of the house, above the first-floor level, was the compromise."[33]

In 1896 Manning left the Olmsted firm, having supervised over one hundred projects yet recognizing that because there were several other men who would always be more prominent in the organization, his opportunities for advancement were limited. He opened an office on Boston's Tremont Street in 1897, with several jobs he had been permitted to take with him.

One of these was for William Mather, who wanted landscape advice for his new summer home, Cliffs Cottage, in Michigan's Upper Peninsula.[34] Because business often required Mather's presence in the north, where his iron ore company had amassed huge land holdings, he had commissioned a modest stone cottage in Ishpeming. The house functioned as a base for extended stays and a setting for a less formal life style than that back in Cleveland. (Charlton, Bilbert and Demar of Marquette, Michigan, were the architects; the cottage was furnished with art and furniture collected by Mather on business trips to Sweden.) In one respect, Cliffs Cottage represented a summertime return to nature, the same impulse—along with the heat—that sent other wealthy midwesterners off to rough it in Michigan's northern woods. But, with its bowling green, stone retaining walls, and fountains, Manning's design for Cliffs Cottage was far more elegant than the average woodland camp. Still, one of Manning's stated goals was naturalism and "plantings representative of all wild flowers" that grew in the area.[35]

Mather hired Manning again in 1902 to landscape the Beech Inn in Munising, Michigan, built to house visiting executives. Eventually Manning would complete fifty-nine separate projects for Mather and the Cleveland-Cliffs Iron Company, including schools, hospitals, mines, and new towns throughout upper Michigan, and, of course, Gwinn.[36]

Manning was pragmatic in his approach to design. He conceived his landscape layouts in direct response to the exigencies of the site and client, tempered by a concern with his clients' emotional welfare, which Manning believed would be improved by time spent with nature. In an address to the Indiana Horticultural Society, "The Purpose and Practice of Landscape Architecture," Manning described the landscape's salutary effects: "The feeble, the sick and those wearied and worn by fatiguing labor, or close application to business or studies, or the excitement and noise of busy city streets, can secure an entire change of scene and be refreshed by the quiet enjoyment of secluded rural landscapes, and the details of the trees, shrubs, and flowers."[37]

Three residential landscapes from Manning's early years—1894, 1897, and 1911—illustrate his artistic development and relate to his work at Gwinn. He was still with the Olmsted firm when he began Walden (named after Thoreau's idyllic retreat) for Cyrus and Harriet McCormick in Lake Forest, Illinois. McCormick took the connection seriously—his awareness that Thoreau "had introduced over fifty new plants into the Concord woods to enrich the flora," Manning later observed, "led him to accept a like introduction of many new trees, shrubs, and herbs."[38] Manning laid out the 103 acres as a wild garden, facilitating views to Lake Michigan and capitalizing on the drama of a deep ravine that ran through the property. (The enthusiastic clients kept the mansion's front hall closet filled with hatchets so they could open views whenever the mood seized them.) Manning worked on the project for forty-two years, until Cyrus McCormick's death in 1936, two years before his own.[39] With Cyrus McCormick, Manning discovered an affectionate and enduring relationship; it was one of many such friendships that grew out of his decades-long wild garden "experiments."

At Walden, Manning discovered that the planning, planting design, and horticultural demands of the wild garden genre were particularly well suited to his talents and philosophical beliefs. He also saw that many of the activities associated with creating and maintaining a wild garden (planting, tree-cutting, and careful observation of nature) offered a spiritual boon to his clients, most of whom led carefully contrived lives, largely determined by social convention. Manning came to see the wild garden as a valuable contribution to the city and regional landscape, especially if it were eventually to become public. Also, even at this early stage in his career, Manning was becoming interested in the aesthetic problem of creating "distinctively American" landscapes. By capitalizing on the existing features of the site, the wild garden celebrated each location's unique American character.

Hill-Stead, in Farmington, Connecticut, begun a few years after Walden, in 1897, struck a somewhat different aesthetic chord and established another kind of estate prototype.[40] Manning probably worked closely on the project with the client's daughter, Theodate Pope (later Riddle), who was collaborating on the handsome house with the architectural firm of McKim, Mead and White. The design Manning conceived for the 250-acre property was quietly revolutionary despite its modest, largely rural look. With assurance and Olmstedian grace, Manning organized the rolling meadows and forest as an idealized American farm; his landscape provided an agreeable, understated, and uncompetitive setting for the house, undoubtedly Theodate's first passion. Hill-Stead marks one of the first appearances of the flexible agrarian idiom in Manning's work.[41] It was the landscape's "archaic spareness," in the words of one landscape historian, that set it apart from hundreds of more elaborate, self-consciously European examples from the period.[42]

In 1911 Manning combined his agrarian and wild garden approach in a more mature, more playful landscape for Frank and Gertrude Seiberling in Akron, Ohio, executed in collaboration with the architect, Charles Schneider. Manning's plan included a winding drive through apple orchard and broad meadow, expansive lawns, a long, narrow terrace with balustraded outlook, formal pool, a walled English garden, a Japanese garden, perennial borders, and two allées (one of London plane tree and one of white birch) extending from the south and north ends of the house. These allées lead visitors from the house to "wilderness" and are themselves both natural and architectural. The site's feature that most excited the designer's imagination, however, was an old quarry—Manning convinced the Seiberlings to buy the property because he was certain that it would make a particularly interesting wild garden. The idealized wilderness he created there not only offered vibrant scenery and varied planting opportunities, but recreation, in the form of swimming, fishing, and boating.[43]

Warm, generous, gentle, and, in the memories of many younger men, father-like, Manning had a happy marriage and stable home life, despite his frequent business trips. He communicated daily with his wife by letter, and with his office by telephone and telegraph, doing most of his writing and designing on the train, between jobs. He was a man of rugged habits and dress, seemingly oblivious to the period's elaborate conventions regarding appearance and behavior. In this respect, he differed from most of his colleagues (not least, Charles Platt), whose more elegant social selves undoubtedly helped attract work. Nevertheless, Manning won the deep affection of many of his clients, including William Mather.

According to one client's account of a typical day at a residential job, Manning arose at dawn so that he might walk the property alone, then breakfasted with the family—still in his hiking boots—and played with the children. He walked and talked a good deal through the day, much of the time about the benefits of donating land to public use, and then retired early.[44] Manning acknowledged that formal socializing did not come naturally to him and later ad-

Platt, Manning, and Shipman   27

mitted that he may have cultivated his rough-hewn image partly "to get a full night's sleep." By avoiding parties, Manning also evaded his clients' friends, who, he once delicately observed, tried "perhaps unconsciously, to gain all the advice from me that they could without paying for it."[45]

In addition to residential, institutional, park, and planning projects—a total of nearly 1,700 jobs at his death—Manning left other, more pervasive influences on the profession. He was among the eleven charter members of the American Society of Landscape Architects and, together with Samuel Parsons Jr., most instrumental in its creation. Manning was a prolific and idiosyncratic writer, addressing topics from plant cultivation to highway design in hundreds of articles for professional and popular publications.[46] His visionary National Plan, a 427-page document, outlined broad reallocations of resources across the entire country. Manning's office gave many practitioners their start: Albert Davis Taylor, Fletcher Steele, Charles Gillette, Marjorie Sewell Cautley, Stephen Hamblin, Helen Bullard, and Dan Kiley were among the many landscape architects he helped launch.

Manning pioneered models for community participation in the design and implementation of public projects; he believed that parks, gardens, and playgrounds designed and built with the assistance of local citizens would naturally best serve local needs. Manning's strong campaign for a national park service during his ASLA presidency in 1914 was a factor in the creation of such an agency two years later. By coincidence, the first director of the U.S. National Park Service was Stephen Mather, wealthy Chicago businessman, avid naturalist, and cousin of William Mather.

On his death in 1938, Manning was remembered in an unusually evocative obituary in *Landscape Architecture*: "Outstanding among the strong traits of his character was his vivid Americanism," noted the writer, and "the vital urge to accommodate a new world to the best uses of mankind .... Mr. Manning possessed an extraordinary power of synthesis. His sense of the unity and glory of the cosmos, including all that was in Nature and all that was in Man as steadily working toward a good and happy end, was almost mysticism. Warren Manning was at heart a poet."[47]

Completing the extraordinary trio of designers at Gwinn was Ellen Biddle Shipman (1869–1950), who was regarded by many of her colleagues, including Warren Manning, as the best flower-garden maker in the country.[48] Her talents extended far beyond the edge of the border, however. At the time of her death in 1950, the *New York Times* identified her as "one of the leading landscape architects in the United States."[49]

Shipman traced the beginnings of her interest in landscape architecture to "a deep love of growing things." She never lost this passion. "One of my earliest recollections," she later wrote, "was the excitement of seeing water that my father had ordered brought for miles to a Nevada [army] post . . . to feed the trees he had planted along the driveways—the only trees in our vicinity."[50]

Born in Berkeley Springs, West Virginia, Ellen Biddle was a vigorous and adventuresome child. She spent her early years on army bases in the West with her mother, father (a colonel), and two brothers. When the fort that housed the family narrowly escaped attack, Ellen's mother took the three children back to Philadelphia to live with her parents. There, Ellen discovered the joys of real gardens. She remembered picking flowers from her grandparents' yard even though

Ellen Biddle Shipman. Division of Rare and Manuscript Collections, Cornell University Libraries

it was forbidden—"a rose to hold all the way to school," she recalled, "seemed well worth punishment."

Shipman attended boarding school in Washington, D.C., where her "great and understanding principal, Miss Sarah Randolph," presented her with an architectural dictionary after catching a glimpse of several house and garden plans in her young pupil's notebook. Miss Randolph, Shipman wrote years later, had seen "deep down below the surface, years before I had realized myself the trend of my mind. It is such seeds that blossom into plants." In many respects, Ellen Biddle's preoccupations did not differ greatly from those of thousands of other young, sensitive girls who loved flowers and gardens and dreamed of beautiful places to live. But a number of circumstances—including, ironically, a failed marriage—propelled her to develop these interests into a career.

Two friendships Shipman formed as a student at Radcliffe College were influential in her choice of vocation. One was with Louise Emory, who married the architectural critic (and Platt advocate) Herbert Croly. The other was with Marian Nichols, niece of Augustus Saint-Gaudens, who helped her uncle design the garden at his Cornish estate, Aspet.[51] Nichols had two sisters: Rose, who became a widely respected landscape architect and garden writer, and Margaret, who married a landscape architect, Arthur Shurtleff (later Shurcliff). Exposure to so many practitioners of the still-obscure art form undoubtedly made it more familiar to Shipman than it would otherwise have been.

In 1893 Ellen fell into an ill-conceived marriage with Herbert Croly's former Harvard roommate, a young playwright named Louis Shipman. The Shipmans and the Crolys visited Marian Nichols's uncle in Cornish that summer and soon grew to love the colony's beauty and artistic rhythms. For the next two summers, they shared a rented farmhouse where the talk often turned to design. The Shipmans made friends with the town's other residents. Ellen was an affectionate and lively hostess, popular in the close-knit community.

Herbert and Louise Croly decided to move out of the farmhouse and build their own residence in 1895. They hired Charles Platt to design it. The Shipmans moved to nearby, less costly Plainfield and signed a ten-year lease on another old farmhouse, this one of brick. Ellen Shipman had a large window installed in the living room and created a robust kitchen-flower garden just beyond. "Never since have I had such marvelous annuals," she later wrote. While Louis played tennis, wrote, and struggled to sell his work, Ellen continued to develop the garden at Poins House—in the process, she discovered the pleasures of gardening and design.

In the winter of 1899, while their house was undergoing renovation, the Shipmans borrowed the summer house of Eleanor and Charles Platt, who wintered in New York City. During one trip home, Charles, who had offered Ellen the use of his studio, discovered some of her drawings inadvertently left on his drawing board. Impressed by the design skill he recognized in them, he surprised her with a "drawing board, T-square and all necessary drafting implements" for Christmas that year. He also left a card on the gift with the message, "If you can do as well as I saw, you better keep on." "My delight was beyond words," Shipman later recalled.

When their lease expired on Poins House in 1905, Ellen and Louis bought a place of their own, not far from the Platts. A growing family and development of Brook Place occupied Ellen Shipman's energies. Brook Place's striking design included a luxuriant perennial garden of peonies, phlox, larkspur, and sharply clipped accents of hemlock. The garden attracted attention throughout Cornish and beyond. In 1924 it was featured in *House and Garden* and illustrated with photographs by Mattie Edwards Hewitt.[52] The article noted that Shipman also considerably modified the house architecture to relate to the new garden.

It may have been because Platt's own talents did not include herbaceous border design—even though his gardens often featured such borders prominently—that he suggested Shipman collaborate with him. She was intrigued by the idea, and undoubtedly motivated to pursue it by the steady decline in her marriage to Louis. She asked Platt for remedial drafting lessons from one of his assistants (which one is not known); the tutoring appears to have lasted about one year.

The first documented commission shared by Platt and Shipman was for James Fenimore Cooper at Fynmere, in Cooperstown, New York, in 1912. By that time, the tax bills coming to Brook Place were in Ellen Shipman's name alone. Louis had continued to prove a difficult and unsupportive partner—gregarious but too effusive, at times manic in his behavior. Later, they would divorce. By 1913 Ellen Shipman, who was probably supporting her three children on her own, regularly identified herself as a professional landscape architect. In 1914 she hired Elizabeth Leonard (later Strang), the first of many assistants, all of whom were women. Although most of Shipman's work during this period came through Platt, she slowly began to find jobs independently.[53]

The Platt-Shipman collaboration paralleled the arrangement of several other male-female teams during the century's early years, when prevailing notions of manliness seemed to depend on near-exclusive involvement with broad design concerns and an avoidance of anything "pretty." Popular wisdom held that women (who were assumed unable to meet the demands of site planning, grading, and large-scale tree and shrub planting design) were more at home in the flower garden. Contradicting this prejudice were high-quality public works by a few exceptionally determined women landscape architects (Beatrix Farrand and Marian Coffin, for example) and the obvious affinity for small-scale details shown by certain male designers (for instance, Fletcher Steele). Interestingly, the prairie landscape style, despite its heavy reliance on native wildflowers, was considered respectably manly, perhaps owing to its implications of large scale.

Differences in training and methodology also contributed to the gendered division of labor. Most architects and some landscape architects created their works on paper, in the Olympian realm of "pure" design; Ellen Shipman and many of her female counterparts approached their work as painters, horticulturists, and dirt gardeners. "Until women took up landscaping," Shipman told one audience, "gardening in this country was at its lowest ebb. The renaissance of the art was due largely to the fact that women, instead of working over their boards, used plants as if they were painting pictures ... as an artist would."[54]

Shipman maintained that deciding what to grow would not necessarily produce a beautiful garden: one must also know *how* to grow it—and revisit the site periodically to monitor the results. In her experience, women understood this better than most of their male colleagues: "I never secure men for any place unless I see it at least twice a year," she told Elizabeth and William Mather when they asked her help in finding a new gardener, "because I have never found any man who is able to keep a garden or place in the condition that I thought it should be."[55]

Shipman's early work, from 1910 to 1920, focused exclusively on planting designs within architectural frameworks established by others—in addition to Platt, she worked in consultation with Harrie T. Lindeberg, Clark and Arms, Delano and Aldrich, Alfred Hopkins, Mott B. Schmidt, James Greenleaf, and Warren Manning.[56] Gradually she came to do more of the overall design herself. A competent site planner and an inventive plantswoman particularly skilled at connecting the garden to the larger landscape, Shipman also designed architectural features, producing work that was consistently elegant and understated. Her gazebos, pergolas, dovecotes, trellises, and garden furniture reflect a quiet originality and an ability to keep the entire garden picture in scale.

Early in her practice Shipman refined an approach to planting design that she never substantially altered. She used plants, "as a painter would," in unexpected combinations that yielded captivating effects of color and texture throughout long seasons of display, relying on fewer flowers than most of her contemporaries. Shipman's debt to Gertrude Jekyll is unmistakable, yet she was no imitator. Her bold planting combinations were innovative and striking—she may have been the first to introduce broadleaf evergreens and conifers into the herbaceous border. Their strong forms provided structure and dramatic texture as a foil for more delicate, transient bloom.[57]

In 1920 Shipman opened an office in New York City and there trained many practitioners. Like her female colleagues, she struggled in competition with male professionals for public commissions. Her few nonresidential projects included the public landscape along Lake Shore Boulevard in Grosse Pointe Shores, Michigan, the Sarah Duke Memorial Garden at Duke University, and Aetna Life Insurance Company headquarters, in Hartford, Connecticut. Shipman completed over six hundred private jobs, however, during a forty-year-long career. Her work took her to Texas, Michigan (repeatedly), upstate New York, New England, and the South, where she designed Longue Vue for Edith and Edgar Stern in New Orleans in the late 1930s. She continued to advise on the estate's development until her death. Among Shipman's other prominent clients were the Algers, Astors, du Ponts, Rockefellers, and Vanderbilts. In 1927 Clara Ford, Henry's wife, hired Shipman to redesign the plantings for Jens Jensen's rose beds near the house at Fairlane. In 1933 *House and Garden* celebrated her "as a sane, understanding leader in her profession."[58]

Ellen Shipman remains a shadowy figure in comparison with her more thoroughly researched male colleagues. Although she frequently lectured—at the Lowthorpe School of Architecture, Gardening, and Horticulture for Women, in Groton, Massachusetts, and to other professional groups and garden clubs—few of her words were recorded. And although her landscape work was extensively documented in contemporary publications, her theories were rarely discussed. Her legacy was further obscured when she donated most of her client-related records to World War II paper drives. And because Shipman's gardens were so labor intensive, most have simply disappeared.[59] But memories of Ellen Shipman linger in the minds of her clients' children and grandchildren. To those much younger, she seemed almost regal in her bearing. Garden owners across the country respected and revered her. Surviving plans, drawings, and photographs record once-splendid landscapes.

William Gwinn Mather

The Muses of Gwinn

CHAPTER FOUR

WILLIAM GWINN MATHER

WILLIAM GWINN MATHER (1857–1951) collected books written by the Mathers who had preceded him. They were a distinguished lot. Richard Mather arrived in Massachusetts in 1635 and five years later produced the first volume ever published in this country, an English translation of the Hebrew psalms. Richard set a compelling example for his descendants—including Cotton and Increase Mather—in the spheres of both religion and book writing. Within six generations the family had produced several hundred volumes and twenty-nine clergymen.

Richard's pioneering spirit survived in his descendants. Samuel Livingston Mather, William's father, arrived in Cleveland in 1843 to dispose of property bought by his grandfather, a charter member of the Connecticut Land Company, owners of the three-million-acre Western Reserve. But after learning of the discovery of precious metals in Michigan's Upper Peninsula, Samuel's interest turned from real estate to mining. He and a group of Cleveland investors hired J. Lang Castles, a scientist from the Western Reserve Medical School, to travel north and conduct his own investigation. Dr. Castles was enthusiastic about what he found, a hill of red dirt "a thousand feet high and a mile long which frightened the Indians because it drew lightning on summer nights."[1] But several members of the group were disappointed, having hoped for more precious metals—copper, or even gold—and pulled out. Still other investment partners lost interest after they went north to see the iron hill and found themselves in wild country surrounded by hostile natives. Samuel, however, was undaunted.

But even more setbacks followed. The company's first mining engineer sent down the devastating news that it would not be economical to process the iron on-site, as originally hoped. The ore would have to be transported via the Great Lakes back to Cleveland, adding considerably to the expense of the enterprise. When, during the financial panic of 1857, the iron mills on the lower lakes were shut down altogether, the number of company supporters dwindled further. But Samuel held on by printing his own "iron money" and convincing his workers to accept and use it. Of the more than one hundred new mining enterprises, the Cleveland Iron Mining Company was one of the few to survive and eventually flourish. Samuel Mather became a very wealthy man.

Samuel already had two children, Samuel Livingston Jr. and Katharine, when in 1857 his second wife, Elizabeth Lucy Gwinn of Buffalo, gave birth to William Gwinn Mather. To house the expanding family, Samuel and Elizabeth built a residence on Cleveland's Euclid Avenue, known locally as "Millionaire's Row."

One of 250 mansions on the world-famous street (praised as a tourist attraction in the 1893 Baedeker's guide to the continental United States), the Mathers' house was located in the same neighborhood as that of Charles Brush (founder of General Electric), George Gund (longtime head of Cleveland Trust Bank, now Ameritrust), John M. Hay (U.S. Secretary of State), Jeptha Wade (director of eight railroad companies and founder of Western Union), and John D. Rockefeller Sr. Many years later, William's half-brother, Samuel, commissioned the last great mansion built on Euclid Avenue. It included two-and-a-half acres of formal gardens, an eight-car garage, and a forty-three-room residence.

Cleveland had gotten its first real economic boost fifteen years before Samuel Mather's arrival. In 1827 the northern section of the Ohio and Erie Canal was completed, transforming the city into the major outlet for Ohio's mineral and agricultural products. By the mid-nineteenth century, Cleveland had a public school system, a public library (one of the first in the world with an open-shelf system), and a large medical center. By 1860 the population had reached 43,500 and hundreds of miles of railroad connected the city with the eastern seaboard, Chicago, Cincinnati, and St. Louis. Industrialization proceeded rapidly after the Civil War. In 1870 John D. Rockefeller Sr. incorporated the Standard Oil Company of Ohio there. No single enterprise, however, led more directly to Cleveland's industrial prominence than Samuel Mather's Cleveland Iron Mining

Company. As this and other new businesses grew, thousands of immigrants flocked to Cleveland for work. By 1900, with 380,000 inhabitants, the city had become the country's fifth largest. Within twenty years, the Cleveland Art Museum, which continues to house one of the country's finest art collections, the Cleveland Symphony, several dramatic societies, the Natural Science Museum, and the Planetarium had been established. William Mather would sit on the boards of most of these institutions.

"Willie," as his grandmother called him, was a bright, hard-working student who showed an early interest in nature. He attended Trinity College in Hartford, Connecticut, where he earned a bachelor of arts degree. After a year abroad in 1877, William became a clerk for his father's company; his duties included inspecting ore shipments at the docks in Marquette, Michigan. He returned to Trinity College in 1885 and received his masters degree the following year.

He then joined the company for good and was promoted to posts of increasing responsibility until 1891, the year after his father died, when William successfully directed a merger with the Iron Cliffs Company and assumed the presidency of the new Cleveland-Cliffs Iron Company. Eight years earlier, Samuel had left their father's company to found a rival firm, Pickands, Mather and Company, which also mined and shipped ore from upper Michigan. Curiously, even as owner of a competing business, Samuel continued to serve as a director on William's board for most of his life—making it impossible, William once remarked, for the board to discuss any real business at its meetings.[2]

The rivalry between William and Samuel remained keen, yet it did not taint their public goodwill toward each other. The high standards of behavior set by their father—and the Mathers before—were strictly upheld by both men. While the two companies were involved in a bitter takeover battle during the 1930s, the brothers vacationed together in Europe.

Over the years, William Mather's company acquired important iron ore reserves throughout the Upper Peninsula, as well as more than six hundred thousand acres of virgin timber, which yielded multiple lumber and chemical by-products. In time Cleveland-Cliffs Company holdings included a 75-percent interest in the Lake Superior and Ishpeming Railroad, several hydroelectric plants, docks in three states, and a fleet of twenty-three iron ore steamers.

Under Mather's leadership and Warren Manning's design supervision, the company built several new towns for its workers in northern Michigan, including Ishpeming, Neguanee, and the "model town" of Gwinn. The first planned community on the Marquette Iron Range, Gwinn was the first anywhere, according to Manning scholar Lance Neckar, that considered industrial housing in the context of environmental planning.[3] Over 8 percent of the town's budget was spent on open-space improvements.

Judged by the standards of his time, William Mather was a visionary employer who provided worker compensation, benefits, and living conditions that far exceeded the norm. He offered prizes for the most artistic and best-maintained homes and gardens. He established visiting-nurses programs and provided rest cottages for convalescent women. He saw to it that "houses were sold at cost to employees, and hospitals and clubhouses established. Landscape artists were employed to make living more attractive, and company engineers pioneered in developing safety devices."[4]

Mather's enlightened ideas about town planning were surely motivated by the rising union movement and his own good business sense, which told him that people work harder and more efficiently when they are happy and healthy. But he also possessed an inherently philanthropic spirit. William's civic record was matched, and in fact exceeded, only by that of his brother, whose fortune also exceeded William's. Both men served on the boards of Cleveland's charitable, artistic, and educational institutions and gave millions of dollars to them. The brothers helped found the Community Chest, which later became the United Way. William was also an extraordinarily generous supporter of the Episcopal church. His million-dollar gift for the new chapel at Trinity College in Hartford more than compensated for his misdeed as a student, when he had carved his initials there and was fined one dollar.

William Mather was not the only Cleveland resident to hire a famous landscape architect during the century's first decades. Between 1916 and 1918 Olmsted Brothers completed two large estate gardens in the city: one for the Harry Binghams and the other for the Warren Bicknells (which won the Landscape Architecture Medal from the Architectural League of New York in 1922). Manning's representative at Gwinn, Albert Taylor Davis, established a thriving practice in Cleveland beginning in 1913. Davis later became an influential writer and one of the country's most highly regarded landscape practitioners.[5]

Another strong horticultural presence in the city was M. H. Horvath, a Mentor, Ohio, nurseryman and apparently self-taught designer who worked on many estates, including those of John L. Severance and H. G. Dalton, near Gwinn.[6] Manning also listed both these jobs on his client list, perhaps indicating a collaboration with Horvath.

Manning first came to Cleveland in 1897 to work for the city's most famous citizen, John D. Rockefeller Sr. He had met Rockefeller years earlier as an Olmsted assistant at Kykuit, Rockefeller's estate near Tarrytown, New York. Manning's involvement at Forest Hill, the Cleveland estate, appears to have been limited to siting the house. Through Rockefeller and other early contacts, including Mather, he was introduced to many prospective clients and eventually worked on fifty-eight projects in the Cleveland area.[7] Ellen Shipman also had several area clients. Prominent among these were the Mathers, the Willard Clapps, and the Windsor Whites. The latter hired her in 1921 to create a formal garden at their estate, Halfred Farms, in Chagrin Falls. Interestingly, Manning also worked for both the Clapps and the Whites. Platt had other Cleveland projects, too, although none residential; in 1911, he designed the Leader Building and, four years later, the Hanna Building and annex.

There was, in fact, enough gardening activity in Cleveland that Platt, when asked to address one of the first meetings of the Garden Club in August 1912, remarked on the need for a unified regional style. "Mr. Platt was most urgent in our gardenwork becoming co-operative," one member noted, "so that certain districts should have similarity and the gardens of Cleveland have a character of a special type so they could be recognized and remembered."[8] Much cooperative gardening did occur under the club's auspices, but a "Cleveland style" never emerged. Gwinn and other fine Cleveland landscapes are best understood today for their individual expressiveness, shaped by time and the idiosyncrasies of their creators and owners.

This is the story of one such landscape.

"First Meeting of the Board of Gardeners, Aug. 3, 1912, Garden Club of Cleveland," Gwinn. William Mather (*left*), Charles Platt (*center*)

PART TWO

THE STORY OF GWINN

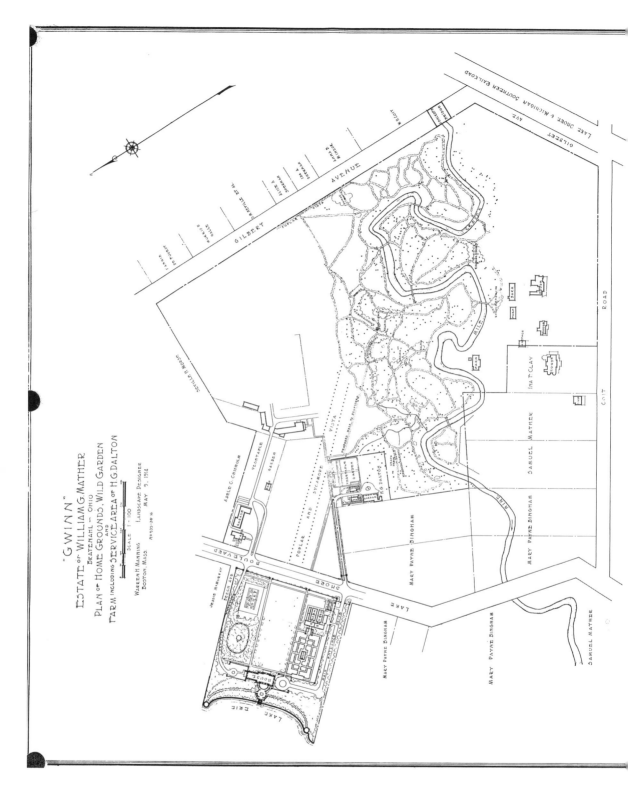

Manning's estate plan of Gwinn

CHAPTER FIVE

LOCATING A SITE

IN 1905, AT AGE forty-eight, William Mather decided to move from the house his parents had built on Euclid Avenue to a location in the eastern suburbs near Shoreby, his half-brother Samuel's place. It did not take him long to find a house he liked, but unfortunately someone else was already living in it and declined to move, despite what was surely a generous offer. Realizing that he might do better to build from scratch, Mather plunged into the process with the same passion and care that characterized his business dealings. It is not surprising that he asked Warren Manning, with whom he had worked before, for advice.

In a letter of 9 November 1906, Mather told Manning that he had found a large building lot he liked. (It was east of the city, not far from Samuel's estate, but not the one he would eventually purchase.) The agricultural area was undergoing gradual development, but the homes were large and attractive and the sense of country, intact.

Manning struggled to remember the piece of land from previous trips to Cleveland; all he could say definitely was that the "proximity of the water with the outlook" was "a very decided advantage." For some reason he seemed more interested in what sort of house Mather ought to build: the "English cottage style," in Manning's opinion, was more "domestic and homelike than any of the types that have been the fad in times past." Because it was just one room wide, easy outdoor access was possible and the gardens could be so closely linked to the house "as to make them practically outdoor apartments of the house itself."[1]

Manning, always pragmatic, went on to advise Mather against using an architect who was too important, too famous, or too expensive because he would not "secure the same personal attention from them or secure as good results for the same cost as...from some younger man." He expressed his enthusiasm for Horace S. Frazer of Chapman and Frazer, who, Manning thought, did "not prepare plans that in the end are likely to cost from one-third to one-half more than the client desires to spend." (Manning's own concern for his clients' financial limits is well documented. Some of the projects listed in his office records were designated "love jobs" and involved no payment at all.) Manning mentioned a few additional, somewhat obscure names; neither Charles Platt nor any other architect of future note was among them.

Manning also suggested some examples of what he considered good landscape design, including the Percival Roberts place, in Narberth, Pennsylvania, designed by Olmsted Brothers, Manning's former employers and current competitors. Ingenuously, Manning noted that he had been asked by the clients to replace the prominent Olmsted firm, and ended by proposing that Mather hire him for the new project, "before you take up this matter at all with the architects."

Mather did not respond immediately to any of Manning's suggestions, including his bid for the job, but continued his search for lots. By 14 November 1906 he had added two more to his list and invited Manning to come west to see them. Manning was a busy man at the time but gave the matter his immediate personal attention. Within five days the landscape architect had been to Cleveland and submitted a six-page report rating the lots on nine characteristics: views, soil, vegetation, shore conditions, location, subdivision potential, garden and lawn potential, and cost. Manning also included sketches of each lot, possible house locations, and some rudimentary garden designs.[2]

Lot A was a pentagon, located at the intersection of Lake Shore Boulevard and Doane Street. Although the site was directly on Lake Erie, the views, in Manning's opinion, were "ragged and unattractive." He thought the "varied, interesting and attractive tree growth" already in place on Lot A its best feature, and the in-town location an advantage, as the estate could provide "an ornament to the city." Manning suggested dividing the property into three parcels, one on either side of the eleven-acre central site, which Mather could retain for himself.

Manning rejected Lot B, adjacent to the Dean Holden estate, as altogether unsuitable for development given Mather's budget and what he had "in mind."

Lot C, the one eventually purchased, comprised two building parcels totaling about five acres between Bratenahl Village's Lake Shore Boulevard and Lake

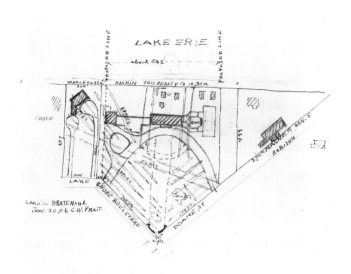

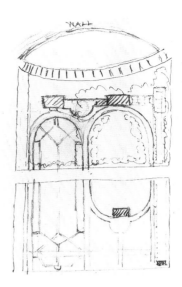

Manning's sketch of Lot A, November 1906

Manning's sketch of Lot C,
November 1906—Gwinn site

Erie. The area was far enough from the city center to escape the noise and smoke, but still within downtown commuting distance—about five miles. Manning was enthusiastic about the views—"directly off to water with no suggestion of shore view up and down the Lake"—and the "amphitheatre–like bluff." He was pessimistic, however, about the potential for horticulture on the site's blue clay soil, which he identified as "cold, wet" and requiring "thorough drainage, deep cultivation, [and an] abundance of manure to put in acceptable condition for lawns and plantation." Neither was the vegetation on Lot C particularly outstanding. "One-third of the lot is open," wrote Manning. "Two-thirds covered with a remnant of the original Elm, Beech, and Maple growth." He continued, "My fear would be not for the beauty of the place, but for the permanence of this beauty, for old trees, like old men, must have a comparatively short life period."

Manning closed his letter with another direct request for the landscape job and an offer to secure competitive sketches from architects that he and Mather could review together, looking for "originality and artistic merit; the men from whose work a distinctively American architecture is developing; not men who are clever copyists and adapters of styles that have grown out of European conditions."

But Mather had his own methods. In January 1907 he asked Manning to assemble a package with more photographs of country houses. Manning sent pic-

Gwinn site before construction, ca. 1906

tures along with varying recommendations for the two lots still under consideration. The photographs featured examples by several nationally known architects. (It is likely that Mather had expressed a specific desire to work with
someone with an established reputation.) Among the projects was Herbert and
Louise Croly's house in Cornish, New Hampshire, designed by Charles Platt.
Manning wrote he admired the house for its "departures in detail that are rather
original and rather distinctively American."[3] The term "distinctively American"
appears seven times in Manning's four-page letter about finding an architect.
Judging from a note Mather scrawled at the end of this letter—"'Indoors &
Out, June 1906' Platt!"—he was eager to find out more about Platt's methods
and work.[4]

By February 1907 Mather had negotiated what he felt was a reasonable price
for Lot C, the Lake Shore Boulevard property—$45,000—although he had not
yet committed to buying it. He was, however, becoming increasingly interested
in hiring Charles Platt to design the house. Mather may have remembered receiving a letter nine years earlier from his friend Charles Freer, a Detroit businessman, about a residential neighborhood Platt was designing for Freer's

business partner outside Detroit, but even a casual look through contemporary magazines would have turned up examples of Platt's work, especially Faulkner Farm and Weld.

One wonders what Manning felt upon receiving a letter from Mather asking him what he thought of Platt's landscapes. His usual effusiveness was nowhere in evidence: "I do not know Mr. Platt personally," Manning answered flatly. "His work, however, I have seen in several places, and I believe that his designs of formal gardens in direct association with the house are perhaps more consistent and satisfactory than any others that I know of." Less enthusiastic observations followed. "The only criticism that I would make in general, is that they are often rather overloaded with architectural objects, and that very often there is not sufficient space for such a display of flowers as the flower lover would most care for. His gardens are usually the architects' gardens," Manning continued, "in which flowers are an incident or rather a decorative feature that is made subordinate to the architectural features. This, of course, is in direct contrast to the flower garden full of flowers in which the architectural features are made of secondary importance and are introduced to give the flowers a proper support or setting, or to make places where persons can enjoy the flowers in comfort." Manning saved what he probably considered the most damaging for last: "I think Mr. Platt prefers to do all the work himself, and that he requires practically a free hand as regards cost."[5] The rest of the letter was curt and offered brief comments on other firms.

Despite Manning's criticisms, Mather's interest in Platt's work continued to grow. He requested references from two individuals, one of whom was a former client. A letter from the Reverend Joseph Hutcheson, for whom Platt had designed houses in 1901 and 1903, advocated vigorously for the Cornish architect, "a most charming man, a gentleman and an artist rather than a businessman," who could "not be bribed into doing what he thought was a bad piece of work because the client wanted it." Hutcheson must have known of Mather's concerns about Platt's fees, for he added, "Mr. Platt does give an unusual amount of personal attention to the work of his office. For that reason he only takes a limited amount of work, and for that reason also he has to charge a ten percent commission, whereas the ordinary architect's commission is, I believe, 5 percent."[6]

Mather received a second, less glowing report. "I have been making inquiries about Mr. Platt," wrote Henry Lloyd Smyth of Cambridge, Massachusetts, "and I find that the people of Cornish have the impression that he is not a very practical sort of person and that he is usually very hazy about costs." Smyth continued, "In the case of one house he built in Cornish the cellar turned out to be too low to stand up in; in another case the cellar always has from a few inches up to a few feet of water in it, and in still another case the stable doors proved to be a little too small to get carriages in and out."[7]

Despite Smyth's blast, Platt got the job, apparently on the basis of an interview in Platt's New York office. Mather then invited the architect to Cleveland to review the two lots still under consideration. At the time, Platt was working for another midwestern client and was able to include Cleveland on a trip already planned, thereby reducing Mather's expenses and economizing on his own time away from New York and his rapidly expanding family.[8]

When Platt arrived in Cleveland in early March, he found a note that Mather, then vacationing in Bermuda, had left behind. He instructed Platt that his house was to include a "large sitting room, parlor, den or office, dining room; and upstairs six to seven bedrooms for family and guests; four of them with bathrooms and of course corresponding accommodations for kitchen arrangements and servants." Mather also left instructions for the landscape plan: "stable and garage accommodations for two horses; three or four carriages, three automobiles. A tennis court, vegetable and kitchen garden and of course principally the pleasure garden."[9]

Platt may not have been disappointed to make his visit to Cleveland without benefit of his new client's company. In a 1912 interview with Charles Downing Lay, Platt claimed that he was usually forced to conceive his schemes "in spite of conversation by husband and wife on irrelevant topics." In the same interview, Platt claimed that the question of style was rarely an issue. In Lay's words, "clients come to Mr. Platt not for a house, but for a Platt house, and these are always in some modification of the Renaissance, be it Italian or Georgian."[10] After reviewing the two remaining parcels, Platt, like Manning, recommended Lot C, though his reasons were different. "I think there is land enough to make something very complete," he wrote Mather. "Nearly all of it is available for treatment which would have a direct relation to the house."[11] The essence of Platt's approach to landscape design was reflected in this assessment; he conceptualized the site, including the house, as a single unit. Individual features within that unit would correspond with one another and with the house, the controlling design feature.

Always succinct—Platt's letters were usually about half the length of either Manning's or Mather's—he got right to the point: he offered to send his engineer to make the necessary surveys of the lakeside property and then to produce some sketches. "I could have something to show you on your return to New York."

Mather responded from Bermuda that Platt should go ahead with the sketches and made his first, and perhaps only, suggestion about architectural style. He said he was inspired by "the light cheerful colors of Bermuda houses" and wondered if it would "be proper to introduce something analogous at Cleveland thereby giving an effect of more color and lightness than is possible with natural brick and stone,—something of the Italian or Riviera effect."[12] Platt approved of his new client's suggestion, it seems.

On the basis of Platt's rough sketch (which does not survive) Mather bought the 505-foot shorefront property in March 1907. He asked Platt for a second, more finished drawing so that he could see the development of the separate areas of the grounds. Mather then turned to the question of budget; he had obviously given the matter some thought. As the land had already cost him $45,000, he wished to limit the rest of his spending (including interior decoration but not furniture) to $55,000.[13]

Platt was not optimistic about Mather's figures. The house he had done for Hutcheson had cost $54,000 three years before, and he estimated Mather's expenses would run at least 10 percent more. Additionally, Platt's rough plan called for a concrete wall around the formal garden and terraces down to the lake "with something in the nature of a sea wall at the end." He estimated that the cost of the proposed garden walls, gardens, tennis court, and outbuildings alone would be about $30,000; the sea wall would add considerably to the sum. "If this figure seems entirely out of the question to you," he warned Mather, "it will be necessary for me to make a much more restricted plan for the house and grounds than the one which I had in mind."[14]

But Mather answered definitively. "I lay more store on the grounds than on the house. I would not want to limit you to the sum I mentioned and which you say is inadequate." Nevertheless, he reminded Platt that he did not want a pretentious house, but one that would "secure its pleasing effect from proportions."[15] Mather went on to request two or three preliminary sketches in different materials and styles that might affect the final cost. The desire for restraint, though motivated by Mather's concerns about budget and Cleveland's perceptions of him, had positive aesthetic consequences. Platt's design was tempered by a moderation that made Gwinn one of his best works.[16]

Before making a more detailed house plan, Platt requested a topographical survey to show the exact conditions at the lakefront and the locations of the trees to be preserved. This he thought could best be done by one of his own men, who knew his preferred methods. Platt considered the lakefront treatment critical to the design success of the estate.

"The key to the situation," he explained to Mather "is the exact position of the house in relation to the lake.... I wish to take advantage of the curve inward which I have observed, and to grade directly from the house to the lake in such a way that the water would be visible from the rooms."[17]

Manning, too, felt that the lake was important, but for different reasons. He saw Lake Erie in Transcendentalist terms, as evidence of the presence of the spiritual in nature: "an ever-changing majestic pageant," he later wrote, "staged by the power that creates and controls the Universe,... multiplied, intensified, and beautified by the waters of the lake. This... beauty gives uplift, inspiration and thrills of pleasure to all whose lives are in tune with the majesties of our unit of the universe."[18]

Manning also appreciated the structural advantages of the curved bluff "formed by hungry Lake Erie's eating blue clay lunches."[19] The cove framed the lake view, screening out any signs of civilization except an occasional ship or plane. The unusual configuration offered a completely "natural" outlook not five miles from a growing urban center. In light of Manning's enthusiasm for nature, it is ironic that his rough site plan placed the house much farther from the lake than Platt's did; his layout would not have capitalized on the lake drama nearly so effectively as the one that was adopted.

For Mather, who used the Great Lakes to transport his iron ore, the water held other, perhaps less poetic associations. From the terrace of the new house, he would be able to enjoy a view of the lakes' largest steamer, the new *William G. Mather*, gliding across the horizon toward Cleveland. After 1906 he might also catch a glimpse of his brother's ship, the *Samuel Mather*, christened a year after the *William G.* and exceeding it in length by a few feet.[20]

In May 1907 Mather wrote Manning to tell him that he had hired Charles Platt to design his new house and he had purchased the five-acre property both men had recommended. He informed Manning that Platt's custom was "to plan the arrangement of grounds as well as the house. But," Mather continued, "in the matter of planting he will seek advice. Mr. Platt and I will both be pleased if you will collaborate with him in this matter. If this is agreeable to you, I will ask Mr. Platt to communicate with you direct on the subject."[21]

Warren Manning responded graciously to Mather's letter. If he was disappointed at not being given primary responsibility for the landscape design, he did not show it. Neither had he entirely abandoned hope for an equal partnership. "It will give me pleasure to collaborate with Mr. Platt, whom you have selected for your architect," he wrote. "It will be my wish and no doubt that of Mr. Platt to have a conference at an early date before his sketches are far advanced, because I am sure that he will feel as I do that neither one of us can consider any of the details of the proposed plan unless each one is in close touch with the other from the beginning."[22]

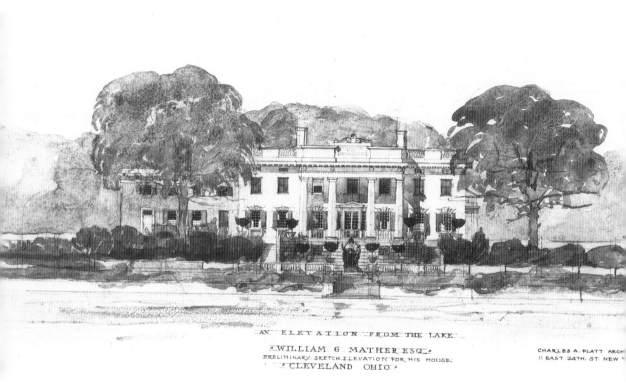

AN ELEVATION FROM THE LAKE
WILLIAM G MATHER ESQ
PRELIMINARY SKETCH ELEVATION FOR HIS HOUSE
CLEVELAND OHIO

CHARLES A. PLATT ARCH
11 EAST 24TH ST NEW Y

"William G. Mather, Esq.: Preliminary sketch elevation for his house," prepared by Charles A. Platt, no date

The Muses of Gwinn

┌─────────────────────┐
│   CHAPTER SIX   │
└─────────────────────┘

DESIGNING THE HOUSE

PLATT'S DESIGN for the Mathers' residence was smaller than many of the architect's other houses, in response to his clients' needs and wishes. In addition to a small servant staff, the principal occupants were to be William and his older half-sister, Katharine, who would act as his hostess and manage the house during his frequent absences.[1]

Two other lakefront residences by Platt, designed almost contemporaneously with Gwinn, offer contrasts to it. The Moorings, the estate of Russell A. Alger Jr., in Grosse Pointe Farms, Michigan, was larger and grander in scale but did not have Gwinn's advantage of a dramatic grade change; the site was only about ten feet above Lake St. Clair. Without the potential for a theatrical descent, Platt chose to emphasize the horizontality of the scheme by placing the house well back from the shore and stretching a broad terrace from it toward the water. This somewhat static arrangement accounts, in part, for the landscape's lackluster effect; although gracious, well proportioned, and elegant, The Moorings does not have Gwinn's dynamism.

At the opposite extreme was Villa Turicum, whose steep and varied lot comprised three hundred acres directly on Lake Michigan. Platt designed the estate between 1908 and 1918 for Harold and Edith Rockefeller McCormick, who rejected plans by both James Gamble Rogers and Frank Lloyd Wright before they settled on him. Platt sited the house at the edge of the lake bluff in almost the same spot as Wright had in his unexecuted plan and almost the same relative

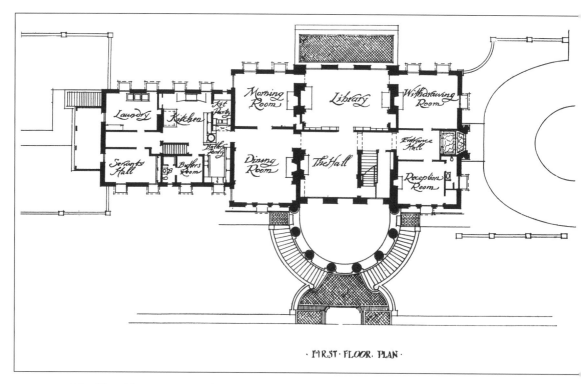

· FIRST · FLOOR · PLAN ·

"First Floor Plan." From Royal Cortissoz, *Monograph of the Work of Charles A. Platt* (New York, 1913)

placement as he used at Gwinn. But where the drop in elevation in Cleveland was about thirty feet, at Lake Forest it was closer to seventy, allowing Platt to create a dramatic descent of stairs, fountains, and terraces. Paradoxically, the huge scale and budget did not serve Platt well: too-liberal borrowings from Italy made Villa Turicum one of his most derivative designs.[2] Gwinn would strike a happy balance between the two.

Platt's plan included sixteen rooms on three floors that in elevation appeared as two—the shorter, little-used third story was hidden by the balustrade at the crown of the house. A two-story wing attached to the east end of the house provided servants' rooms upstairs, a large kitchen and service areas downstairs.

Visitors would enter through a door located on the short (west) end of the house. Two small rooms—a reception room (later William's office) to the left and a withdrawing room (later music room) to the right—flanked the ample entrance hall. A walk through the entrance hall would bring visitors to a wide staircase on the left. Beyond this was a large hall where, through a wall of windows, the spectacle of the lake would be revealed. In the Italian tradition, the grandest view was hidden and then offered with a flourish.

Directly across the hall, a large library let onto a covered terrace and a broad, tranquil view of the front lawn. Later this view would be enlivened with the planting of a poplar allée across the boulevard. Moving east, through the hall, visitors would next come to the dining room; to the right was a morning room. A butler's pantry stood at the end of the hall and, through it, the kitchen, laundry, servants' hall, and other, small service rooms. The east door opened outside onto the service court. Platt's design for the house was stately, even monumental, yet the rooms were intimately proportioned and free of heavy applied detail.

The most unusual feature of the house was its placement: as close to Lake Erie as feasible. (During one violent winter storm giant waves reportedly hurled fish against Gwinn's upper-story windows, where they froze and stuck overnight.) Platt capitalized on the lake drama by creating a semicircular portico on the north house facade. From this vantage point, accessible through French

Music room, Gwinn, no date

doors in the hall, visitors could experience the lake yet still have overhead protection. The large stone columns that supported the roof had the interesting effect of structuring the lake view—framing it, as it were, so that it became an abstraction, a Whistleresque work of art.

The portico was a quotation from that most American building, the White House. Two terraces lay below it, joined by double curving flights of stairs. The plan did not spring full-blown from Platt's imagination: in June 1907 he changed the shape of the portico from a circular to a semicircular shape; an earlier watercolor sketch shows it as a square. "This is a better composition from all points," Platt wrote about the final scheme, "and it materially helps the effect which I tried for from the start, that is to make the house appear to be directly on the lake." He reiterated this intention when he described the design for the sea wall, the purpose of which was to "cut off distance between the house and lake."[3]

Within days of buying the property, Mather had located a local engineer, General Jared A. Smith, experienced in shoreline construction. But high waves prevented Smith from making the soundings Mather thought necessary before

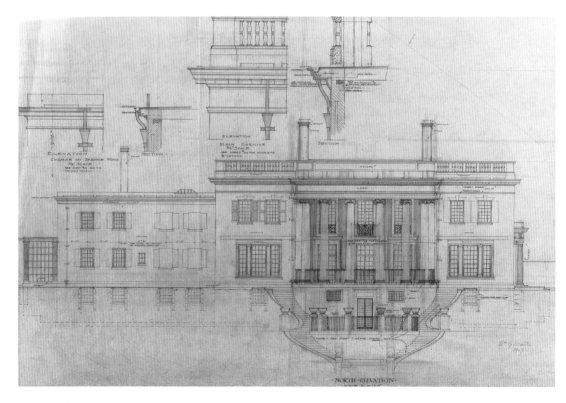

"North Elevation," prepared by Charles A. Platt, 1907. Charles Platt Collection, Division of Drawings and Archives, Avery Architectural and Fine Arts Library, Columbia University in the City of New York

The Muses of Gwinn

Gwinn site after amphitheater grading, 1907

the physical and financial feasibility of Platt's plan could be settled. Mather wrote Platt asking for more information about his proposed plan. He told Platt that he wanted all the lakefront work completed before winter and the house construction far enough along so that work could continue through the winter, noting that, at age fifty, he could scarcely afford to postpone moving in. (He actually would live to enjoy Gwinn for another forty years.) By July, Smith had secured the necessary information from Platt and proposed two alternatives for the lakefront treatment, a breakwater and a retaining wall. Platt favored the drama of a wall, which would literally embrace the water.

The previous month, Platt had sent Mather yet another set of plans, which included the addition of a billiard room under the portico and larger servants' rooms—both at Mather's request—and an overall increase in cubic feet from 177,000 to 200,000. The estimated cost of the house had climbed to $80,000, or forty cents per cubic foot. Four days later, he sent a new estimate, suggesting a total cost of $146,500, not including the purchase price of the land or the sea wall, the feasibility of which was still being studied—about three times the initial budget proposed by Mather. Yet another revised estimate, which arrived three days later, shaved $4,000 off the cost of the house but added $1,000 to the steps from the house to the lake, perhaps in response to new information from the engineer.

Designing the House   57

Increasingly uneasy, Mather wondered whether they might not save some money by using one of the downstairs rooms as a bedroom, but said he hesitated to suggest changes "because the plan as a whole pleases me very much, and the general style of the exterior (with its corresponding interior) seems so suitable to the location.... Nevertheless," he continued, "I am afraid of the cost.... we have [still] got to furnish the house, and, although I would be careful not to have it in the slightest degree extravagant, yet, while keeping it as simple as possible, it should be commensurate with the dignity and style of the house and will necessarily consume [considerable] money."[4]

Mather soon resigned himself to the unanticipated expense, however, and dove into the design process with relish, reviewing the development of every plan in daily letters to Platt. (One wonders about Platt's initial reaction to his client's "hands-on" style; eventually they would become good friends.) Most of Mather's letters included a barrage of questions. That of 10 July 1907 was typical: Was there going to be enough light in the servants' hall? Why were there steps up into the main hall from the back hall? What had become of 1.5 feet in

Upstairs hall, Gwinn, no date

The Muses of Gwinn

the transition from one drawing to another? Was it not a mistake to eliminate the east windows of the two guests' rooms? Would the laundry be better off located in the basement? Would there be a convenient cellar for the furnace?

Incredibly, by mid-July 1907 Platt had decided on all aspects of the house plans except the south porch. "I will change it entirely," the architect wrote, "and make a one story porch with columns same as those at the front door, arranged so that glass sashes may be put inside of the columns in case you wish to use it as a conservatory in winter."[5] But this scheme would also change. Mather said he did not really care about the exact design of the porch, as "it was an afterthought."

He did, however, want Platt to arrange to come to Cleveland soon. He was tiring of the many administrative and artistic questions he felt were properly Platt's domain. "I feel as if I had more than I want to do in arranging for the specifications and contracts for both the shore protection and foundation work," Mather wrote his architect.[6]

Platt was juggling several commissions at the time and, as sole principal, was eagerly pursued by all his customers. He responded to Mather's complaints in the formal language that would soften over the years into warmer tones. "I re-

Construction of fountain terrace, 1907

Designing the House   59

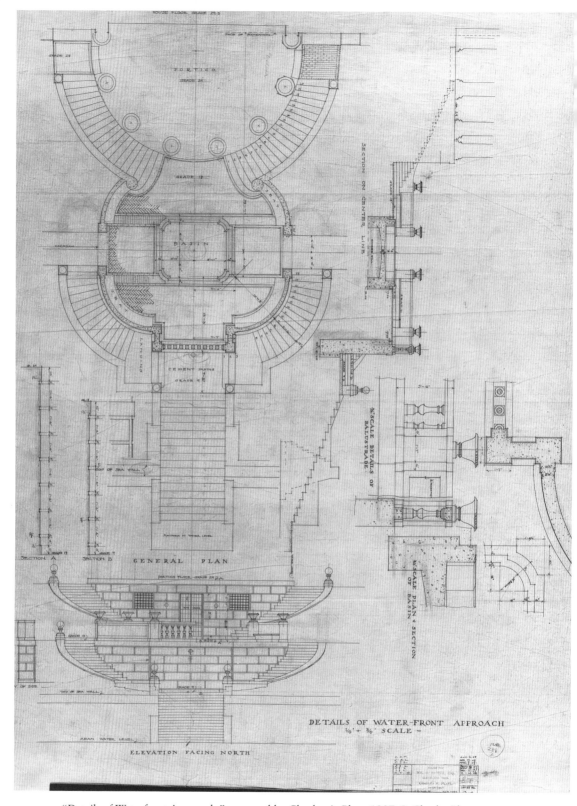

"Details of Waterfront Approach," prepared by Charles A. Platt, 1907–8. Charles Platt Collection, Division of Drawings and Archives, Avery Architectural and Fine Arts Library, Columbia University in the City of New York

gret that it will be impossible for me to come out to Cleveland just now, in fact for some little time and I think my presence there at a later date will be more useful."[7]

The geographic distribution of architect, client, and contractual workers plus the complexity of the project rendered Gwinn an extremely ambitious operation. Daily letters and telegrams kept the network of Mather, Mather's secretary (Charles G. Heer), Platt, Platt's engineer (F. H. Henderson), and various contractors and subcontractors in constant contact. Several local architects, including Abram Garfield, Dercum and Beer, and Bohnard and Parson, were also used for purposes of supervision and, in some cases, to design buildings. One memorandum, from 13 January 1909, lists fifty-nine workmen representing thirteen different contractors at work on the estate that day.[8]

Once the foundations were complete, the house walls went up quickly. But Mather continued to make suggestions about the house interior as construction proceeded. No detail was too small for his attention. "I want to get everything in my house as convenient as possible," he wrote Platt. Among the items he suggested were a temperature-controlled wine cellar, a plate warmer, upstairs and downstairs silver safes, a central vacuum "plant," glass windows for kitchen cupboards, hinge lockers ("as they have on shipboard instead of a place for a flour barrel"), cold storage, electric call buttons for servants, and the exact locations of radiators.[9] Within a few weeks, Mather submitted a long list of features he had recently observed at "a charming villa" in Thomasville, Georgia. These included mirrors fitted into bedroom doors, automatic electric lights in closets, hooks on bathroom doors for shaving straps, bathtubs filled from spouts instead of from intakes on the bottom, sinks in servants' rooms, laundry tubs in the center of rooms and so accessible from all sides, and wash basins in bedrooms.[10] Platt approved all of them, except for the laundry tub locations and wash basins, which he thought impractical.

In the winter of 1908 Platt sailed for Europe with his wife and bought the first round of furnishings for Gwinn, including chairs, tables, chaise longues, commodes, cupboards, seats, and desks, most of it in the style of Louis XV. He also purchased china, tapestries, linens, paintings, vases, mirrors, mantelpieces, and stone benches in Paris, Venice, Bologna, Florence, and Naples.[11] Platt looked to Emil Feffercorn, a New York decorator, to supply fabrics for upholstery and window treatment.

Platt explained his approach to interior design to Mather. "I have no drawings which give the color schemes, and it is not my custom to make them as I have found that they give very little in the way of a correct idea of the contemplated treatment. After deciding in a general way what treatment will be necessary in the different rooms, I leave the color schemes to be worked out according to what may be obtained, and the longer this may be left, the better, as I often get valuable suggestions by standing in the rooms when they have reached a certain point of completion, as to whether light or dark colors should be used upon the walls, and the scale of figure to be used in the wall covering, and all details of that kind."[12]

In this way Gwinn's interior evolved over the years, furnished with a mixture of the antique and the new and an eclectic collection of paintings, tapestries, and prints, most of which were purchased according to Platt's recommendations. (Platt did not charge a commission on "pictures above the grade of decorative"—including the Corots, Dewings, and many others Mather bought on his recommendation. "I feel that I get as much fun as you do out of the process of buying them," he wrote Mather, "perhaps more, because I do not have to pay for them.")[13]

Gwinn had begun to coalesce, inside and out, into an organic unit. In the minds of the designer and client, it was becoming a work of art.

Library, Gwinn, no date

The Muses of Gwinn

CHAPTER SEVEN

DESIGNING THE
GARDEN

PLATT PLANNED Gwinn's home grounds at the same time as the house—together they formed an integrated composition. Terraces, porches, lawns, and garden rooms allowed for easy access from indoors to out and from one garden area to another. Exterior spaces reflected the proportions of the house, which served as a controlling element for scale as well as placement of other features. The deceptively simple layout set up a varied sequence of movement through the landscape. Big, open sunny spaces contrasted with more intimate shady spots. Disappearing paths and half-glimpsed vistas would gently draw visitors through a series of shifting scenes and offer a range of different experiences—in the Italian tradition.

Notions of comfort and variety were not limited to Italy, but Platt considered the gardens he had studied there exemplary in these respects. In Italy, Platt wrote, the garden offered the opportunity to "walk about and find a place suitable to the hour of the day and feeling of the moment, and still be in that sacred portion of the globe dedicated to one's self."[1]

Platt's ability to envision views from one garden area to the next served him well at Gwinn. The lakefront terraces provided a frame for the great watery expanse beyond; the broad front lawn invited glances from within the more dense-

Aerial view to northeast, ca. 1950

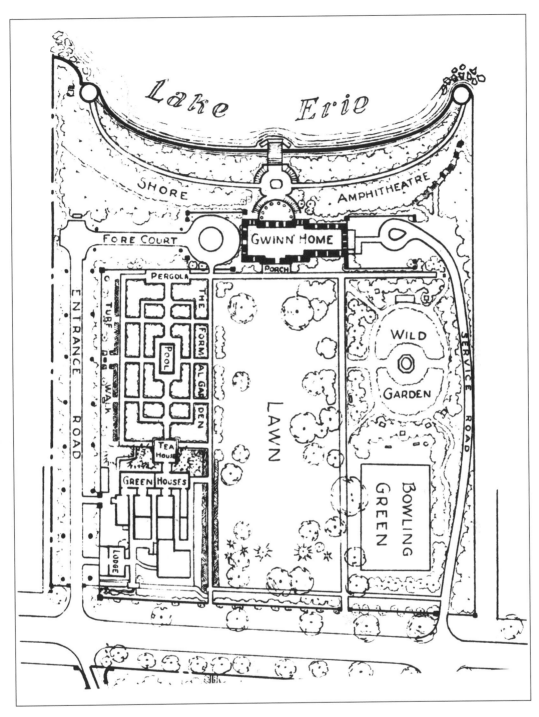

Labels within the plan:
Lake Erie
Shore
Amphitheatre
Fore Court
Gwinn Home
Porch
Pergola
The Formal Garden
Pool
Turf Walk
Tea House
Green Houses
Lodge
Entrance Road
Service Road
Lawn
Wild Garden
Bowling Green

"Gwinn" (detail), Plan No. 935-59-2, prepared by Warren H. Manning Offices, Inc., 13 January 1931

ly designed areas flanking it. Views from the house interior were also carefully crafted: landscape vignettes were visible from every room.

The structure of Gwinn's landscape was determined largely by the use of architectural elements, although Platt took his cues for the location of specific areas from existing features, primarily the lake and the grove of mature deciduous trees on the east side of the front lawn. Plantings would be integrated into the elegant "bones" of the architectural determinants to soften and, in some cases, accentuate them.

Visitors arrived via a driveway running north from Lake Shore Boulevard, along the western boundary of the rectangular property. A righthand turn at the end of the drive led to a large forecourt and the formal entrance to the house. The entry drive was mirrored on the east side of the house by a similarly routed service drive that conducted deliveries to the service court. The service court was screened to the north and south by masonry walls.

Lake Erie bounded the property on the north, embraced by the long, curving, concrete sea wall ending in platforms that eventually would support gazebos. A series of terraces and steps connected the house to the lakefront. Manning later

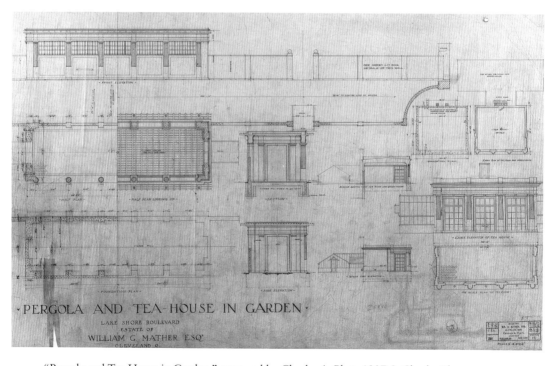

"Pergola and Tea-House in Garden," prepared by Charles A. Platt, 1907-8. Charles Platt Collection, Division of Drawings and Archives, Avery Architectural and Fine Arts Library, Columbia University in the City of New York

The Muses of Gwinn

Construction of teahouse, greenhouse foundations, and gardener's house, view across formal garden, 1908

wrote admiringly: "Mr. Platt's intent to not let the house slip into the lake was made evident by the deep-set concrete crescent wall with a stone walk at its back, a concrete apron at its water-washed toes, and with columned gazebo outlook shelters at each end. At this wall's center, steps passed up from the water's edge between two sleepy stone lions to the lower fountain terrace, and then to the portico at the main floor of the house."[2]

On the south side of the house, Platt's design broke the expanse of land into three distinct, roughly equal areas: a large central lawn, visible from the library, flanked on the west by a formal garden with central pool, pergola, and teahouse and on the east by a wild garden, or bosco, sited to take advantage of the existing grove of trees. South of the formal garden, and hidden from it by the teahouse, were greenhouses, cutting gardens, and the gardener's house. South of the wild garden, a tennis court was planned but probably never executed. Later this was the site of a bowling green and then a grove of exotic trees described in one document as a "collection."

Warren Manning did not become actively involved in planting at Gwinn until the summer of 1908, a full year after construction on the house and waterfront terraces was begun, and after most of the architectural determinants were in place. Manning's charge from Mather— "to advise" Platt in matters of planting—was an apt description of his role early in the project, but it soon became apparent that Manning's horticultural expertise would be needed to create areas

Designing the Garden   67

Formal garden under construction, view toward lake, 1908

Formal garden after planting, with George Jacques, ca. 1909

of distinctive character throughout the estate, to locate plants and suggest substitutions when original choices proved unattainable, to salvage existing trees, and to prepare the difficult soil for new trees and shrubs, many of which were large. Over time, Manning's role was even further expanded.

Mather described to Manning the overall effect he sought for Gwinn, "the element of what might be called grace and personal charm.... In other words, avoid stiffness and coldness." But photographs reveal that Gwinn's emerging landscape was far from graceful. Newly constructed architectural forms loomed bleakly out of bare terrain. Broad, still-unplanted areas looked ragged and forlorn. In September 1908 Mather wrote to both his designers that he was "anxious" about his landscape and reminded them that he wanted to avoid the "effect of coldness and lack of individuality." His goal for Gwinn, Mather confided to Platt, was "the personal charm and grace of the old English garden." He mentioned Hampton Court as a model.[3]

Only Manning responded in writing to Mather's worries; perhaps Platt reassured him over an evening of bridge (both were avid players). While Manning emphasized his general support for Platt's "rigid design" and guaranteed that it would be softened "with a graceful and attractive drapery of foliage and flowers," he also reminded his client that the plan was Platt's, not his. Regardless, Manning pledged his loyal support in helping Platt "in every way I can to make his design a successful one."[4]

Entry drive after first planting, ca. 1908

Entry drive with mature planting, ca. 1925

Manning suggested that Mather visit a selection of American gardens to gather more ideas for his own place. Among those he mentioned were Platt's Weld, the Larz Anderson estate in Brookline, Massachusetts, and one of his own projects, done in conjunction with the Olmsted firm, for Mrs. J. C. Hoagland at Seabright, New Jersey. Manning said he thought the best informal gardens were those of Charles Sprague Sargent, also in Brookline, which Manning did not design, and the Thayer estate, in Lancaster, Massachusetts, which he did. Manning warned Mather, however, against imitating any of these gardens. He thought the key to a great design was originality. "If your place is to have the personality that you wish it to have, it must grow out of your own taste and the taste of your advisors." Manning went on to say that the feature at Gwinn which appealed to him "most strongly and will give the place the greatest distinction is the treatment of the great amphitheatre" and added, "The gardens will be distinguished from other of Mr. Platt's gardens…by less of the piling of architectural detail which architects so like to include."[5]

While most of the horticultural decisions at Gwinn were ultimately left to Manning, the entry drive was a true collaborative effort. It was Platt's idea to use a double row of American elms to create a high arch. Manning concurred, explaining to Mather that elms would balance the large mass of tall trees on the east lawn and—always practical—pointing out that they would be easy to locate, transplant, and grow.

The understory scheme for the drive was Manning's design. "I have planted a nearly continuous mass of the native Viburnum dentatum or Witherod," he wrote to Mather, "because it has good foliage, grows well in shade, will face down to the turf in an attractive manner, is attractive in flowers and fruits, is free from disease, and can be secured in good sized plants." For variety, Manning mixed in a few *Viburnum Opulus* (cranberry bush) but limited the palette because he knew visitors would experience it from inside moving cars—details would be blurred and a wide mixture would produce a choppy effect. Manning explained that the effectiveness of the driveway planting "will grow out of the lines of Elm trunks and their overarching branches, the continuous belts of dark green Viburnum foliage and a deep shadow formed at the end by a covering of Euonymus under a canopy of over-arching Birch foliage."[6] Manning's plant choices for the drive, and throughout Gwinn, were informed by an awareness that the landscape would be seen year round. (In addition to spring flowers and autumn color, viburnum have berries through most of the winter.)

For the end of the drive, Manning planned a grove of white birch and Scotch pine. The latter, he said, would "take on a picturesque outline, simulating to some extent that of the Swiss Stone Pine." *Betula papyferis* were later replaced by gray birch when many of the original plants died; Mather suggested a change from Scotch to white pine, which he thought would do better on the exposed site. Mather's interest in plants and gardening, stronger than Manning's typical client, contributed a valuable, local perspective to discussions about plant culture and design.

Manning's planting under the birches and pines included raspberry, maple-leaved viburnum, *Hydrangea arborescens,* 150 *Hydrangea nivea,* 500 Teabush (*Ceanothus americana*), 1,000 Yellowwood (*Xanthorrihiza apiifolia*), and 100 'Sweet Briar' roses. The unusual combination offered delicate, idealized woodland effects, especially under the white trunks and dappled shade of the birch.

North portico after grading, 1908

North portico, after 1910

At Gwinn, Manning relied primarily on native plants for his design framework but mixed in exotics for a longer and bolder floral show than native species usually deliver.

One of the most challenging areas Manning had to plant was the curving slope of the lakeside amphitheater. For this he chose Japanese barberry "because it is doubtful if any other plant could be found that would be more attractive," and "thick matted roots…will hold the surface from washing." The barberry gave a richly upholstered texture to the sweeping curve; the leaves were green until autumn when they turned a dazzling scarlet-orange.

To flank the stairs down to the lake, Manning ordered white fringe, a showy native shrub, also known as "Daddy gray-beard," which sports unusually delicate

South porch, doors to library, undated

West gazebo with apple tree, after 1912

74

West façade and forecourt, 1908

West façade and forecourt, after 1912

blooms in late May. If "suitable plants of sufficient size" could not be secured, Manning suggested substituting a "plant having similar foliage."

Manning indicated stands of Lombardy poplar (*Populus nigra* cv. 'Italica') on either side of the portico, at the southwest corner of the house, and the northwest corner of the pergola in the formal garden. He knew that the poplars would not live more than twenty years but chose them anyway, assuming that they would be replanted as the need arose. Their quick growth and shimmering forms could not be duplicated by any other tree and were needed to break up the insistent flatness of the site. The trees' similarity in silhouette to the spires of cypress that punctuate the Italian countryside was surely not lost on Manning or Platt.

Formal garden, privet bays, looking north, no date

The Muses of Gwinn

For the ends of the two curving shore walks, Manning at first suggested "a tree of medium growth with horizontal branching... probably the White Mulberry" to overarch the gazebos. Later, an equally picturesque apple and golden bark willow were substituted.

Where the driveway made a right turn to approach the house entrance, the American elms were discontinued, but the broad proportions of the roadway were maintained as it terminated in the forecourt. (A planting was initially considered for the island in the center, but a circular fountain eventually occupied it.) Manning used large groups of lilacs and mock orange (*Philadelphus virginia*) to screen the garden wall to the south and the lake to the north. He suggested Japanese wisteria at each corner of the house and old-fashioned coral honeysuckle on the trellises at the door. Later, in the interest of reduced maintenance, this scheme was formalized with clipped *Taxus*. The front lawn planting incorporated the existing maple, oak, and elm trees and added more of the same.

Platt took sole responsibility for the planting plan of Gwinn's formal garden. Given the exceptionally close relationship between the complex architectural framework and the plants within it, Platt convinced Mather that the same office should design both. The formal garden plans bore the signature of Paul Rubens Frost, who spent just one year, 1908, in Platt's office. An excellent horticulturalist, Frost soon left to pursue an apprenticeship with Olmsted Brothers.[7]

Frost's plan for the formal garden used California privet (*Ligustrum ovalifolium*) to create buttresses along the west wall. These "should make pleasant bays," Mather wrote back approvingly, "a secluded alley for a stroll between said hedge and wall." He told Platt that the lack of nooks and crannies in the overall scheme had bothered him and he was relieved to see a few at last. "It should be our aim," Mather argued, "to provide such secluded spots so that in the survey of the grounds from the house, the eye will not be able to take in all the points of interest in one glance. There should be surprises in store for one who strolls around and which are not perceptible from the house."[8]

Platt's plan also called for specimen flowering trees and shrubs centered in the nine bays created by the privet buttresses. Crab (*Malus Halliana*), white fringe (*Chionanthus virginicus*), dogwood (*Cornus florida*), silverbell (*Halesia carolina*), and redbud (*Cercis canadensis*) were underplanted with roses, mostly perpetual hybrids. The walls behind the bays were draped with vines, including *Euonymous*, Baltic ivy (*Hedera helix*), *Clematis jackmanii*, *Akebia quinata*, Virginia creeper, *Parthenocissus quinquifolia*, and several varieties of climbing roses, including 'Farquhar,' 'Multiflora,' 'Dorothy Perkins,' 'Dawson,' 'Rubiginosa,' 'Harrisons,' and 'Ballinore Bell.' The effect was full, rich, overbrimming.

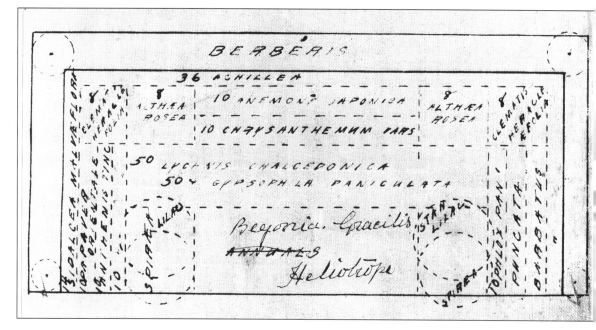

Formal garden planting plan (detail), prepared by Charles A. Platt, 24 July 1908

Mather seemed happy enough with the plantings in the bays but was disappointed with Platt's initial proposal for the herbaceous borders in the sixteen central beds. "I presume you expect to have in another place... provisions for annuals, roses and bulbs," he wrote with some impatience. "So much space devoted to perennials [tends] to monotony."[9]

Platt responded to Mather's criticism immediately. (It is difficult to believe, yet true, that in 1908 the U.S. mail was often delivered between Cleveland and New York within twenty-four hours.) "The planting plan which you have seen," wrote Platt, "was incomplete as it was hurried off to give your gardener an idea of the seeds that he would need to plant now. I have modified the plan very much since then and provided places for annuals." But in the revision Platt had apparently taken the matter of annuals too literally to heart. Mather wrote once more to say that he thought Platt had gone overboard, and asked for more space for perennial delphiniums, foxgloves, and some hardy lilies.[10]

A week later, Platt adroitly sent back two plans for Mather to choose between. One alternative offered many annuals; the other reallocated some of the annual space to roses. Mather may have been expecting Platt to exercise the same decisiveness in planting as he had in architectural matters—but balustrade profiles seemed to make more compelling topics for debate. Platt's relative lack of involvement in planting design is reflected in his closing sentence to Mather: "The general effect of the garden will not be materially affected either way."[11]

Despite the apparent nonchalance, Platt's, or Frost's, final plan was meticulously detailed. It called for perennials in geometric, concentric bands within the beds, the centers of which were to be filled with annuals. Most of the plants flowered in June and July in a palette of blue, yellow, and white. The overall pattern was also symmetrical—east and west beds were paired. *Veronica, Achillea, Coreopsis, Delphinium, Aster, Helenium, Polemonium, Nicotiana, Gypsophylia, Iris, Phlox, Penstemon*, sixteen standard lilacs, and 1,600 individual barberry shrubs (*Berberis Thunbergii*, for hedging) were listed, together with about forty-five additional perennials and annuals.

In the summer of 1908, as discussions unfolded about what to plant where throughout the estate, it became apparent that Manning was not particularly interested in flower borders either. They were fundamentally alike, Manning explained to his client, "in that you must use ... practically the same flowers that are used successfully in other gardens." This ubiquitous palette of hybrids, he observed, had been cultivated to "conform to certain garden standards that all tend toward uniformity of character and outline." Wildflowers, in Manning's view, however, were another matter. "Here by a careful selection of varieties,"

Figure 34. Rhododendron and wildflower groundcover of original wild garden, no date

View through lilac arch to formal garden, ca. 1913

he wrote Mather persuasively, "you can secure the choicest of woodland effects, grouped in such a way as to secure a certain amount of formality without destroying the grace, the intricacy, and the charm of uncultivated plants."[12] Mather liked the sound of grace, intricacy, and charm, and gave Manning sole jurisdiction over the development of Gwinn's wild garden.

The small bosco on the northeast quadrant of the front lawn was the answer, in both Platt's and Manning's eyes, to the geometric formality of the flower garden opposite. Manning felt strongly that its wild character should be maintained. His plan called for large groups of *Rhododendron maximum* and *catawbiense* tall enough to provide seclusion and shade. These were to be collected in the wild.

To cover the ground, Manning suggested "shade loving plants that [would] retain a good foliage throughout the summer." Among these were waterleaf (*Hydrophyllium appendiculatum*), wood violet (*Violet palmata*), Indian and California strawberry (*Fragaria indica* and *Fragaria californica*), lily-of-the-valley (*Convallaria majalis*), trillium (which "would give very attractive flowers in their season, then lose their foliage"), creeping Jenny (*Nepeta glechoma*), lungwort (*Mertensia virginica*), mistflower (*Conoclinium*), *Hepatica*, and a variety of ferns, "to give a succession of flowers during the spring and summer."[13] Manning reeled off the wildflower names as though they were old friends, but it is doubtful that Mather had heard many of them before—nor was he prepared for the subtlety of their effects. The wild garden scheme would metamorphose several times before he was content.

The Muses of Gwinn

Once plans were worked out on paper, Manning's challenge was to locate plants of the size and quality that would give the desired effects as quickly as possible. He was one of the first landscape architects in the country to practice plant collecting on a grand scale. Many of these hunts took place in the mountains of North Carolina, where rhododendron grew in abundance and where Manning was working on several projects in association with the Pinehurst Resort. Nonetheless, finding just the right plants for Gwinn proved a challenge. In November 1908 Manning wrote to Mather that he was searching in vain for "plants with character."[14]

One of his best discoveries was a large group of mature lilacs on an old estate in Brookline, Massachusetts. "I have been watching this lot for a long time," he explained to Mather, "hoping I might have a place for the plants as they were rather unusually good and in sufficient quantity to make up a carload."[15] Manning used one hundred of the plants to create a boundary between the lawn and the formal garden. Trellis arches between the clusters permitted glimpses from one area to the other.

In this case—not an isolated one—the availability of plants had actually influenced design. It took flexibility and imagination to envision appropriate places for discoveries that were not part of the original plan. It also took a certain tact and business aplomb to pull off the transactions gracefully since not everyone welcomed inquiries about plants growing in their own backyards.

Despite massive new plantings, in autumn of 1908 Mather complained that Gwinn still looked dreary, owing, he thought, to a lack of evergreens and colorful deciduous trees. Manning reassured his client that the somber tones were, in part, the result of an unusually dry season. But Mather would raise the issue again the following year, and the one after that, when weather conditions were better.

In truth, Manning's taste in planting design was more subtle than his client's, which had been shaped by the Victorian plantings up and down Euclid Avenue. Even among landscape architects of the period, Manning had an unusually sensitive appreciation for the mauves, beiges, and russets of fading elm and oak leaves.

In 1910 Mather wrote to both Manning and Platt about adding new trees to the front lawn; he was considering introducing evergreens. "A couple of splendid, fully-developed spruce at each corner, with wide spreading branches near the ground, would be ideal" he told Manning.[16] Mather had just returned from several months in Europe, where he had visited many distinguished—and old—gardens. He was unsettled by the lack of maturity of his own place.

South façade and lawn, ca. 1913

South façade and lawn, ca. 1930

Entry to drive, gardener's house with George Jacques and unidentified woman, no date

Manning responded quickly. "I can hardly answer this intelligently. It seems to me that you have rather more variety in the foliage ... than one would expect on a small place, on account of the old trees ... that have established by reason of their age a character that gives distinction to the individual as well as the group." He reminded Mather that "it was this group of trees and the established character that comes only from age that led me to recommend this site to you originally." (This, of course, was not completely accurate—in fact, Manning had warned Mather that the trees might not live very long.) Manning was clearly put off by the idea of blue spruce on the restrained "American" front lawn of Gwinn. "The blue form [of Colorado spruce] is so pronounced that it seems to me rather obtrusive in a lawn."[17]

Eventually, Mather and Manning struck a compromise in the form of groups of quick-growing native white pine to fill the corners of the lawn. The billowy, soft green trees satisfied Mather's need for additional fall color and Manning's sense of appropriateness.

In the late fall of 1908 Manning sent his representative, Albert Davis Taylor, to oversee planting at Gwinn. Taylor was to help Mather's ground superintendent, George Jacques, "hunt elms, big shrubs, and groundcover plants" in the Cleveland area, including the ravines belonging to another of Manning's Cleveland clients, Jeptha Wade.[18] The rivalry that often existed among Manning's, and other designers', clients usually did not prevent them from helping one another in this way.

Only the most trusted assistants were sent out to supervise important commissions like Gwinn. Manning's success at running a large practice stemmed primarily from his ability to train able younger practitioners, like Taylor, quickly and then give them the authority necessary to succeed in the field. They were responsible for communicating their boss's ideas to the superintendent of the estate, who would oversee planting and maintenance year round. Taylor was one of Manning's most valued representatives, yet Manning encouraged the young man to strike out on his own. He later wrote, "It was obvious that his individuality was so marked that his best work would come from an office of his own in which he would be dominant rather than as an associate with other practitioners."[19] As Olmsted had, Manning permitted his protégés to take jobs-in-progress with them when they left.

Of even greater importance to the long-term success of an estate was its superintendent. Gwinn's first, George Jacques, born and trained in Britain, was a highly accomplished, although not particularly artistic, flower gardener with a penchant—as Ellen Shipman later discovered—for red geraniums. Jacques had been hired at the beginning of the Gwinn project and grew with the job, adapting his vocational identity as a gardener to an expanding set of tasks. It is unlikely that his former employment, whether in the United States or the United Kingdom, included much plant hunting.

CHAPTER EIGHT

REFINEMENTS

AS THE WINTER OF 1909 ebbed into spring, William Mather got his first real look at his newly planted landscape. He was no happier with what he saw than he had been the autumn before. The planting seemed thin in many places, and the surfaces of the walks in the formal and wild gardens were unfinished. By the end of June, he wanted to move into the house, but it dissatisfied him, too. It seemed "a little cold and bare," he later wrote Platt—the same criticism he was making about the landscape.[1] A huge planting campaign was set for the fall, but first the material that had been heeled-in the previous autumn needed to be placed.

Warren Manning had been through the process many times before and was optimistic in the face of Mather's dark mood. "Things are getting in shape at your house," he enthusiastically wrote his client after a trip to Cleveland in April. He told Mather he had helped with the planting himself and that he was going to return again before it was completed "to add to the refinement of detail that I am anxious to secure."[2] Manning thought that the new plants had come through the winter very nicely and noted that George Jacques was doing a good job.

But Mather was disappointed in the operation and with Manning's less than rigorous working methods. He pointed out that there were still sizable holes in many areas of planting because some of the orders had not been placed early enough to obtain certain plants. He told Manning he wanted a plan on paper for the coming fall's planting. He also reiterated the collaborative agreement

Path between original wild garden and lawn, no date

with Platt: "I trust you will commence early enough with your drawings and designs for the completion of this planting to give ample time for a thorough consideration with Mr. Platt and me on the subject before it is time to order them. In this way we will have our ideas thoroughly digested."[3] By spring 1909 Charles Platt's role in the planting design had been defined for the long term: his opinion, even in horticultural matters, carried weight.

Manning still had sole responsibility for the wild garden, and drew up a long order of new items for the area. His list was sent not to a nursery but to Arthur Harrison, one of his field superintendents overseeing new mine-related projects connected with the Cleveland-Cliffs Company in the Upper Peninsula. Manning asked Harrison to locate, collect, and package several thousand plants—all of them northern Michigan wildflowers—and get them aboard a Cleveland-Cliffs iron ore freighter bound for Cleveland.

Manning explained the order to George Jacques in characteristic, somewhat romantic detail: "200 Clematis verticillata. This is the native large-flowered, pale

The Muses of Gwinn

blue clematis, and this I would have planted in places where it will scramble over Rhododendrons and low shrubs in light shade. It is not a rampant grower like the Clematis paniculata, neither is it as rampant as the Virgin's Bower, so it can be used safely in our wild garden." He continued, "I have ordered 100 sq. ft. of each of the following: Cornus canadensis (Bunchberry), Pyrola in var., May Flower (Epigaea repens), Clintonia boroalis, Polygala pauciflora. These are all shade loving plants that can be planted under the branches of Rhododendrons and in the bare spots of the garden." Manning indicated that these plants were to be sent in sods that could be broken up and spread out to cover an even larger area. He was apparently unconcerned that Jacques's time and effort might be spent putting in plants whose prognosis for naturalizing in Cleveland was slim: "Of these varieties the Epigea may not succeed for any length of time, but it is worth while to have it even if it only succeeds and gives flowers for one season."[4]

"I have ordered 100 Prenanthes which will grow from 3–5' high and should be planted at points where they will push up through low shrubs in the wild garden," Manning went on. The order specified 50 plants each of *Epilobium angustifolium, Petasites palmata* (Japanese butterburr), and *Aralia nudicaulis*. It also called for 200 each of two ferns, *Aspidium marginale* and *spinulosum*, 100 *Polystichium Braunii*, and 200 *Cystopteris bulbifera*—"varieties that you do not have there, the first being quite rare." The list finished with 1,500 violets, 500 *Hepaticas*, 100 square feet of *Clintonia borealis*, and 100 *Eupatorium ageratoides*.

In the same letter Manning also sent instructions for planting and descriptions of preferred habitat. "Please do not attempt to limit yourself to the wild garden in finding a place for the plants," he directed Jacques. He wanted groundcover everywhere, as it would be "more attractive than bare earth."

On 25 September 1909 the Cleveland-Cliffs Iron Company steamer *Centurian* left Marquette, Michigan, carrying twelve crates of wildflowers in addition to its usual load of 16,000 tons of iron ore. When it docked in Cleveland several days later, few suspected that the ship had any purpose so delicate as transporting violets.

Mather told Manning that all the planting on the estate was to be finished by late fall that year. Mather was sailing on a four-month European vacation in December and he wanted things settled before he left. So on 10 September 1909, Manning, Mather, and Platt met at Gwinn to discuss changes and additions to the plantings. After long discussion, several decisions were made. Manning's notes on the meeting ran to twelve typewritten pages.[5]

Pan figure in original wild garden, no date

Bust in original wild garden, no date

Existing plantings of lilacs (in the forecourt) and rhododendrons (in the wild garden) were to be supplemented with smaller plants to add heft and to screen leggy plants. Jetbead (*Rhodotypos kerriodes,* now *Rhodotypos scandens*) was ordered in two sizes to give "a good facing down [of lilacs] to the turf line" of the big lawn.

Manning indicated that the massed groups of rosebay rhododendron (*Rhododendron maximum*) inside the wild garden were to be bolstered with leather-leaf (*Cassandra calyculata,* now *Chamaedaphne calyculata*) and bog rosemary (*Andromeda Polifolia*). Both evergreen members of the heath family, they would enjoy the moist, acid environment Manning had created. Another 175 rhododendrons were to be added: 50 scarlet for the lawn side, 50 crimson for the tennis court side, 75 mauve and purple for the north edge. This level of detail is comparable to the refinement of line and color in a painting that occurs as the artist builds the composition, necessarily, layer by layer. Manning clearly expected to return to his planting plans again and again, refining and in some cases re-defining his original ideas. It was not dissimilar to Platt's ongoing development of the house interior.

Manning ordered eighty small maples (*Acer platanoides*) added to the pleached allée in the formal garden, which was not growing fast enough to suit Mather. The allée was a significant structural feature. It extended the east walk in the formal garden and separated the cutting gardens and greenhouses from the lawn. Eventually, the entrance to a large wild garden across the boulevard would align with it.

To fill an area between the service drive and tennis court site, Manning suggested that a belt of trees be increased with ten flowering dogwoods (*Cornus florida*), five red-flowering dogwoods, two Tartarian maple (*Acer tartaricum*), five cypress, two sour gum (*Nyssa sylvatica*), two sweet gum (*Liquidambar*), ten *Syringa reticulata* (five of which were weeping tree lilacs that proved unavailable), five Golden-rain trees (*Koelreuteria*) and several mountain ash (*Sorbus americana*) transplanted from Negaunee, Michigan. These were all small, ornamental trees, each exotic in its own season, selected for their interesting display and late autumn color.

One thousand square feet of huckleberry sod were ordered from northern Michigan to be used on the lower edge of the Japanese barberry amphitheater planting. A later experiment for this area involved tawny daylily (*Hemerocallis fulva*), but neither planting succeeded because of the waves that sometimes crashed over the sea wall. Eventually Manning gave up and went back to the barberry, which offered a clean, almost abstract sweep of color between the

Forecourt with mature plantings, no date

light, curved wall and the dark, green allée that was planted behind it in 1910.

Manning tried moonflower (*Ipomoea alba*) on the lampposts along the shoreline walk to the belvederes (it also failed, however). Six dead American elms on the entry drive were identified as needing replacement. Manning suggested adding tulip poplars (*Liriodendron Tulipifera*) to the lawn planting; he argued that they were readily available and "quite as free from disease as any tree we could select." Neither Platt nor Mather liked the idea initially, but Manning eventually won them over.

They also discussed the treatment of the formal entry on Lake Shore Boulevard. "Would not a pair of deciduous cypress trees in plain turf, with vines draping over the wall and posts be good?" Manning asked. Mather agreed, and the mixed planting was removed in favor of the simpler vignette.

Fragrant honeysuckle (*Lonicera Morrowii*) was ordered to face down the tall viburnums along the entrance drive and the lilacs in the forecourt. Manning's formula for the new planting was less casual than the effect would suggest: "I will order 50 Snowberry to go with Lonicera morrowii, these to be used sparingly on the main drive, to be increased in the road to the forecourt and to make up about one-half of the facing down of the lilac groups in the court, the other half to be made up of a few Lonicera morrowii, the balance to be Rhodotypos kerriodes. A few separate bushy plants are to be planted irregularly along the wall on the north side of the court."[6]

One of the biggest design challenges on any estate job was how to achieve graceful modulations from one plant group to another. Manning made these sometimes invisible, sometimes startlingly beautiful, transitions seem almost inevitable. With his vast plant repertory and his thorough understanding of how plants grow in nature, he had become a master of horticultural segue. Manning once likened his approach to that of the painter who "uses his pigments, to secure certain landscape effects. He does not select a plant for a position because it is rare, but because it gives just the shade of color, texture, or outline to complete the ideal picture he has formed in his mind."[7]

A clash over the plantings for the curving amphitheater walks brought Manning's romanticism and Platt's classicism head to head at the meeting. Manning was openly opposed to Platt's French suggestion "of using little pyramids, such as might be made by trimming an Arbor vitae." His own preference was for edging the walks with "irregularly rounded trees like the dwarf Black spruce." Manning explained that he anticipated the spruces taking on "rounded cushion-shaped forms from wind exposure."[8] He particularly liked the idea of the irregular growth recording the patterns of wind and waves over time.

"The only distinctly formal incidents here are the walks and lanterns," Manning continued, "and we decided, I believe, to have a drapery of slender vines over these lanterns. These will then be submerged in the general rounded outline." Manning said he had emphasized the informality of the shoreside planting by choosing pachysandra instead of grass to edge the walk and irregular, picturesque trees ("leaning Apples and fleecy foliage Willows") to shelter the pavilions. "For all these reasons," he concluded, "I think it would be better to have the cushions of dark color that the dwarf Spruces will give rather than the cone shaped trees."

Mather, however, did not like either suggestion and postponed the decision until the following year, when he announced to his designers that he had made up his mind to plant two curving allées of Norway maples, an idea suggested "by the charming alleys" he had seen in Italy, north Germany, and Switzerland.[9] In this instance, Mather was at his administrative best, synthesizing extremes to produce an artistically successful compromise. The maple allées were both romantic and classical. When pleached, *Acer platanoides* strike a geometric note

View (east) through Norway maple allée, after 1910

yet retain their natural lushness; their foliage glistens in the rain and flashes in the wind; early spring chartreuse becomes deep green in summer and then amber as the season ends.

In 1909 Platt began work on a design for the interior of the teahouse, a small building that bordered the formal garden on the south side. The little garden structure was first conceptualized as a place to overwinter the garden's tender bay trees, but another building, part of a farm complex across the boulevard, would soon serve this purpose. Mather's suggestion in August 1908, that the building be made into a palm and fern house with a glass roof, proved unfeasible. It may have involved more money than he wanted to spend.

In Platt's new scheme, the teahouse was redefined as a glass-enclosed parlor, a place to socialize in the garden regardless of the weather. An enclosed building also offered the potential of interior murals, a characteristic Italian feature and one Platt had used with success in his own Cornish garden. In July 1909 Platt wrote Mather that he was sending along drawings of a Pompeiian scheme for the murals. He proposed that the painting be done by J. Alden Twachtman, son of Platt's friend the painter John Twachtman. The colors, Platt indicated, would have to be decided on-site, but the details could be worked out in full-scale

Wall painting in teahouse by J. Alden Twachtman, 1993.
Photograph by Carol Betsch

drawings before the actual painting began. Mather had mixed feelings about Platt's figurative program. He thought it "a little exotic" and suggested instead that "a frieze or border to the panels, of a flower or vine design—say grape vines or climbing roses or some other flower design, would be more appropriate to the locality than a strictly Pompeiian design."[10]

But Platt was persuasive, and soon nymphs, satyrs, cherubs, and all manner of mythological creatures were sporting playfully—and amorously—across the dark red walls of Mather's teahouse. Bold green and turquoise borders framed the large figures; a lower course of cherubs frolicked with satyrs, goats, and chariots beneath a trompe l'oeil molding decorated with lions' heads. Against the dark blue ceiling the signs of the zodiac were surrounded by garlands and winged creatures—Pegasus, swans, and a group of Tritons riding on dolphins. Lighting strips, later improvements, were recessed behind a wall molding near the ceiling. They illuminated the whimsical scenes with a modernist twist.

The greenhouse structure was designed by the well-known specialists Hitchings and Pierson shortly after the initial house and garden construction was complete. It was, however, an anticipated component of the estate from the beginning. The layout responded to many of Jacques's and Mather's suggestions for convenience and ease of maintenance, including a raised lily pool that could be covered and used as a bench in summer when the plants would be outdoors and the use of slate instead of wood throughout the interior to prevent rot.

In December 1908, as the greenhouses neared completion, Mather placed an order with Thomas Rivers and Son, in England, for sixty-two plants, most of them fruits for pot culture. Listed were peaches, nectarines, apricots, cherries, plums, and grapes along with ornamental flowers, including orchids, and ferns. Fan-trained peaches and nectarines were also ordered for planting in the cutting gardens to the east and south of the greenhouses. In 1913 an addition expanded the available space to almost nine thousand square feet, including the workroom

Greenhouses, 1993. Photograph by Carol Betsch

and propagating house. The annex comprised melon, rose, strawberry, cucumber, and chrysanthemum houses.

With its lush plantings and patterned tiled floor, the greenhouse offered a tropical respite from the bitter cold of a Lake Erie winter. But the impetus for expansion was not primarily aesthetic; it was Mather's pleasure in having year-round fruits, vegetables, and cut flowers (one newspaper report mentioned "orchids, crimson begonias, and hundreds of roses").[11] Mather enjoyed a bowl of strawberries in January in much the same spirit as a walk on his terrace on an August evening: by 1909 it had become clear that a quest for life enhancement was propelling design development at Gwinn.

Mather decided that he also needed a cow stable and a new building "on the back lot" for Jacques's tools, wagons, and horses. The previous year, several additional acres had been purchased when it became obvious that not all the service buildings would fit onto the original grounds. Mather asked Platt to design the new buildings, but Platt was too busy and suggested that the work might be

Farm group south of Lake Shore Boulevard, 1993. Photograph by Carol Betsch

The Muses of Gwinn

Apple allée and chauffeur's cottage (*left*), no date

done instead by the local Cleveland firm of Dercum and Beer. Platt volunteered to review their plans and discuss possible changes with his long-time client and, now, friend.

The new structures took their architectural cues from Gwinn's main house, gardener's cottage, and chauffeur's house. Owing to their less imposing scale and vernacular qualities, they were, perhaps, even more charming. Vegetable fields, orchards, and meadows added to the picture of agricultural bounty and village atmosphere. The "back lot" had become a little piece of Italian countryside.

The buildings were linked, at Manning's suggestion, by an apple allée on axis with the chauffeur's house on Lake Shore Boulevard and the garage group behind. The allée separated two rectangular vegetable gardens. Behind them was the building cluster, which eventually included chicken coops, a chicken yard, cow stable, bay tree house, farmhouse, and farmhouse garden. A small fruit garden, a "farm woods," and a place for more vegetables and grapes sat still farther in from the street. The new development, including the long field at the eastern edge of the woods, covered several acres.

In 1914, when the buildings were almost complete, Mather began to search for a farmer to live there full time. "I don't know whether you ever act as employment agent," he wrote Manning playfully, "but I am in need of a gardener who will raise for me the nicest vegetables that are raised in this country; asparagus such as you get at Monte Carlo; beans such as you get at Nice; peas such as you get in Paris; chickens such as you get in Cafe de Paree; and also knows how to handle cows. In other words, is a first-class gentleman's gardener.... He ought also to have a good looking wife," Mather continued, "who knows how to make butter and will keep a nice house and board a chauffeur and a house man."

Manning teased in response: "When it comes to such a man as you are looking for I am afraid his wings are so far developed that he is twanging his harp in the gardens of the hereafter.... Why do you insist that his wife should be good looking?" he continued, perhaps genuinely befuddled. "It seems to me that a good looking man is more of an ornament to the place because he is likely to take his place among the garden statuary more frequently."[12]

Vegetable garden and farm group, 1993. Photograph by Carol Betsch

The Muses of Gwinn

CHAPTER NINE

TAMING THE WILD GARDEN

ON 11 DECEMBER 1909 Mather sailed for Europe on the steamship *Berlin*. During the five-month trip he visited Paris and Venice, where he shopped for the house and added to his collection paintings by Marieschi, Barozzi, and a sketch attributed to Guardi. In Italy he also visited gardens. When Mather returned, Platt gave him some of his own photographs of Italian gardens, probably taken on his 1892 trip, and one of his etchings. Inspired by the trip, Mather immediately began to plan for improvements at Gwinn. On 17 May Manning left for his own "medicinal" Mediterranean tour. He departed from Boston aboard the S.S. *Romantic*, bound for Gibraltar, Naples, and Genoa.[1]

In autumn, all three men turned their attention to Gwinn's wild garden. In response to Mather's increasing discontent with the area, Manning suggested the addition of several new plantings to broaden the variety of bloom and texture. He proposed low care but flamboyant lilies, including *Lillium davuricum*, *elegans robuste*, *tenuifolium*, *speciosum*, and *superbum* (Turk's Cap Lily). The splashy blooms marked a departure from the subtler spring display that resolved into a uniform green groundcover by June.

But Mather was still unhappy about the garden's appearance. "It seems to me to lack character," he explained to Manning. "One walks into it with the feeling that he is going to see something particularly attractive, but there is a measure, to me at least, of disappointment. It is indefinite. I think there should be more interesting features; places, for example, where one would sit and enjoy a particularly charming spot, with perhaps a distant view."[2] It is not clear what this view might have included since the lake was not visible from this point and Lake Shore Boulevard was at most two hundred feet from it in the other direction.

Manning was quick to defend his design. "The principal reason why you are disappointed in the wild garden," he wrote Mather, "is that you have not had an opportunity to see it at its best. Such a garden is most attractive in the spring"—when Mather was often in Europe, California, or Bermuda.[3] Manning also pointed out that he could not secure the character he was after without trial and error as it was impossible to predict accurately which plants would thrive in the quantities necessary to make an impact.

He then appealed to Mather's ego, explaining that the design was for "the comparatively few people who can fully appreciate the ... quiet tones of green and inconspicuous flowers" contrasted "with brilliant masses of color that you can get in the open flower garden." Manning continued, "Seats and other objective points will interest those who have not a sufficient knowledge or appreciation to enjoy the little things that appeal to the one who has a knowledge and love of woodland flora." Finally, Manning noted his occasional conflicts with Jacques, who "does not know well and probably does not care much for the wild garden." Manning ended his long letter with a direct challenge: "I believe that you will find that this garden will grow upon you in interest even more than the flower garden as you watch it through the year."

But Manning must also have felt compelled to offer tangible improvements because he suggested two amendments to the original design: a set of cast concrete stepping stones and a series of small bronze fountains. He sent two sample stepping stones—one imprinted with leaves of red oak, the other, with gray birch—and indicated he had a model of a trumpet vine fountain ready. The fountain, according to Manning's description, was about three feet high with a twenty-inch basin to be set on a boulder; moisture from a constant drip would encourage the growth of mosses and algae and make the surrounding earth damp enough to grow other wetland plants. Manning suggested that several of these be made, along with one or two seats that would also be based on native plant forms. But Mather's response was lukewarm.

Manning was unaware that Mather had simultaneously contacted Platt with the same complaints. "I fear it is not large enough so that the spaciousness of it would compensate for the lack of individual features.... I think when one walks

100   *The Muses of Gwinn*

· ELEVATION ·　　　　　　　　· SECTION ·

¾ & F.S. DETAILS OF FOVNTAIN · IN · WOODS ·-TWO-SHEETS

"3/4 & F.S. Details of Fountain in Woods," prepared by Charles A. Platt. From Cortissoz, *Monograph of the Work of Charles A. Platt*

through it," Mather continued, "there should be particular features where one would naturally be inclined to sit and enjoy them—a vista, or particularly attractive planting, or a little formality of one kind or another."[4]

In response to Mather's concerns, Platt proposed a monumental Italianate fountain for the garden's center, a single ornament that would transform the area's indeterminate character into a dramatic setting with its own distinct identity. Manning's transcendent love of nature may have appealed in theory, but Platt's solution showed the greater awareness of what was needed in a purely visual sense. Mather commissioned Manning to create a version of the wildflower fountain for his garden at Cliffs Cottage in upper Michigan.

Platt had turned to several sources of inspiration for his fountain design. The bronze finial at the top was based on that of the Fountain of the Moors at the Villa Lante, one of the world's best-known formal gardens. The dolphins appear to have been adapted from the Giusti garden outside Verona. (There were also dolphins on a new fountain for Gwinn's formal garden, but the Giusti model, whose dolphins overlapped the bowl they supported, more closely resemble the wild garden composite.)[5] Piccirilli Studio in New York was commissioned to carve the figures to Platt's specifications.

Taming the Wild Garden　　　101

Fountain in original wild garden, 1957. Photograph by Walter P. Bruning

In April 1911 the stonecutters Blum and Delbridge of Amherst, Ohio, were given quarter-scale models of Platt's design "to be strictly followed," according to instructions from his office. Further communications, though, were apparently rather vague. "A man appeared at my place this morning," Mather wrote impatiently to Platt in mid-April, "telling Jacques that he had a contract to put up a fountain. He had no blueprints with him, did not know where the fountain was to go, and altogether it was rather blind. However," Mather continued, "he said that some of the pieces composing the fountain weighed five tons, so I presume it is the one intended for the grove."[6] (During the period, several other fountains were also under construction at Gwinn.)

Figuring out where the fountain should be placed—Mather hired his own engineer to pinpoint the exact center of the woods—was not the only hitch in the operation. It soon became apparent that a great number of plants would have to be removed to provide a track for the steam-run derrick to unload the big pieces of stone. Jacques, who had been diligently planting the area for the past three years, resignedly reversed course, fully aware that he would soon be putting the plants back in the very spots he was digging them from.

Fountain in original wild garden, 1957. Photograph by Walter P. Bruning

It took the gardening crew two weeks to spade out and ball-and-burlap the rhododendrons and the wildflower groundcovers. While Mather was waiting for the foundation people to begin their work, he had yet another idea: on 1 May he wrote to a company in Darien, Connecticut, for information about peacocks, but the birds never materialized.

Mather also asked his designers to consider a new planting scheme for the wild garden, since he was now anticipating an expanded role for the area as a setting for dinner parties. Manning, as was his custom, prepared a long report; Platt's suggestions were not recorded. Manning recommended using only ground-cover plants that could withstand foot traffic. Primary among these, in his opinion, were moneywort (*Lysimachia Nummularia*), Indian strawberry (*Fragraria Duchesnea*), and "such low and tough leaved plants as Hepatica, Barren Strawberry, Fringed Polygala, Pyrola and Wintergreen."[7] Ferns and other brittle plants were to be moved elsewhere. Manning proposed that some of the exotic plants introduced by Jacques, including pachysandra and hydrangea, be removed as they looked "out of place." In this same report, however, Manning suggested introducing an evergreen ivy (*Hedera helix*) that was no more native than pachysandra or hydrangea. The first planting did not do well, but subsequent attempts were so successful that the Baltic ivy eventually crowded out everything else except the spring bulbs.

Manning thought that the squill (*Scilla siberica*) had looked particularly good the previous spring and recommended another five thousand for the October planting. He also suggested adding one thousand each of glory-of-the-snow (*Chionodoxa luciliae*) and star-of-Bethlehem (*Ornithogalum*). He hoped that the tiny delicate blooms would naturalize but planted them in large enough quantities that they would make at least a moderate impact in their first season. Manning was not being extravagant; the total cost of these seven thousand bulbs in 1912 was $25.50.

In 1911 a boxcarload of mature hybrid rhododendrons was purchased from an estate in Pennsylvania to thicken the failing *Rhododendron maximum* in the wild garden. Manning must have realized that the plants would never be happy in the cold clay soil, no matter how many tons of leaf mold were worked into it or how many drainage tiles were installed. In fact, the rhododendrons and humus would have to be replaced about every seven years—their maintenance became, in effect, an extended bedding-out practice. But Manning had no good alternatives to the rhododendrons, one of the only evergreen shrubs that would survive under the tree canopy. Before they began their decline, their broad, glistening leaves, mid-summer bloom, and loose, graceful growth habit were just what the romantic woods required.[8]

Conversations about improvements to Gwinn's wild garden continued between Mather and Platt even after the big fountain was in place. In 1914 Mather was still trying to persuade Platt to work up suggestions for additional "refinements." He was not adamant, he said, that the improvements be architectural; nevertheless, he went on to suggest a little pavilion that would offer a "warm, sunny shelter."[9] He tried to get Platt to give more attention to the project by pointing out that Gwinn could become an important showcase for the architect. "These extra touches which we are now contemplating should pretty nearly finish the construction work on the place and make it a distinctive and attractive example of your work in this direction."

But Platt's services were in great demand. "It will be some time, I am afraid," he replied, "before I will have anything to send you." By the following spring, however, he had designed two sandstone seats for the wild garden, and soon had another inspiration. "I have just had offered me six columns of which I enclose a blueprint," he wrote. "These are in old Verona marble, and might be just the thing for the arrangement you suggest back of this seat. [They] can be had

Pergola in original wild garden, 1993. Photograph by Carol Betsch

Taming the Wild Garden   105

for $700.00. I would suggest having them sent out and sticking them up in a temporary way to get an idea of the space you want them to enclose. Connection by some woodwork on top to carry vines could be arranged after it had been determined how much space you wanted the feature to occupy. The columns are 8'7" in height, which I think would be about right." Platt thought the Verona marble, "yellowish red and comparatively low in tone," would harmonize well with the sandstone of the seats and the big fountain nearby.[10]

Platt's suggestion—that Mather's gardening staff "stick up" the columns in a temporary way in order to experiment with the dimensions of the new pergola—was not his typical design approach. But time, or the lack of it, seems to have kept the architect from getting more involved. He may have made a trip west to review the arrangement of the columns and set the final spacing, but no record of it survives. The feature soon took its place at the north end of the bosco, not far from the wall that separated the area from the service court.

Platt's evolving design for the wild garden echoed the arrangement in the formal garden: each had a large fountain in the center, pergola at the north end, and stone benches placed throughout. Later that year, small stone "terminal" figures were sited among the greenery in the wild garden to perform much the same design function as the well curb and stone orb in the formal garden: interesting incidents, not immediately apparent on entering, they lent charm to the garden and broke up the monotony of the massive plantings.

The wild garden was much improved by the architectural additions; it seemed even more like the craggy, romantic shadow of the formal garden opposite. But it did not and never would provide the wilderness Manning longed to create and Mather would come to love. A different source for that would be discovered across Lake Shore Boulevard.

CHAPTER TEN

THE FOUNTAINS
OF GWINN

IN ONE YEAR, 1911, William Mather was going to spend more money on plantings, paintings, sculpture, and fountains than he had once contemplated spending to build the entire estate.[1] Financial success at Cleveland-Cliffs Iron Company made the new work possible, but Mather was equally motivated by his excitement about Gwinn and its potential as a work of art.

The sound and sparkle of water transformed Gwinn's static elegance into a more musical landscape composition, joining previously disparate garden areas into an integrated whole. The ironwork gate to the formal flower garden was also completed at this time; the distinctive turquoise "Gwinn green" trim made a lively contrast with the sandy garden walls, whose tone matched the stucco house. New sculpture was designed, too.

A pair of life-size sandstone lion-sphinxes resembling those flanking the entrance to the Villa Medici in Rome were carved by Piccirilli Studio in New York. The crouching beasts were to flank the flight of steps leading to the lakeshore. Not thinking to indicate to the contractors which way they were to face, Platt was surprised to hear from Mather that the cranes had arrived but the operators did not know if the animals were to go end to end or head to head. Situating the lions on a north-south axis, facing, or not facing the water, would have left someone, either Mather or approaching boats, with an awkward view.

Entry gate between forecourt and formal garden, 1957. Photograph by Walter P. Bruning

"Lions on Sea Wall" (detail), Sheet No. 108, prepared by Charles A. Platt, 29 July 1910. Charles Platt Collection, Division of Drawings and Archives, Avery Architectural and Fine Arts Library, Columbia University in the City of New York

Mounted on their plinths facing each other—as Platt intended—the lions seemed to be guarding the depths beyond.

A bronze figure of a cherub modeled after Verocchio's *Boy with Dolphin* was set into the center of the new square pool on the north terrace. The figure could be viewed from the portico above, silhouetted against the vast lake horizon, or seen from the steps below. Frolicking against the horizon, the happy putto further dramatized the spareness of the water panorama.

A second fountain, the "Old Man" (according to family memory), was set into the curving wall of the portico foundation. Although the classical prototype for the ram horned figure has not been determined, the grape vines suggest Bacchus. The wall fountain was hidden from view, discoverable only after descending one of the curving staircases from the portico.

In the forecourt, the circular traffic island was fitted with a low basin with a central jet. Small lion's heads spouted water from the basin's edge; exotic lilies grew within.

The formal garden was also undergoing changes. Platt added a life-size bronze copy of *Fortuna*—cast by Tiffany and Company—to the rectangular reflecting pool at the garden's center. Again, Platt looked to Italy for his source; *Fortuna* stands in the Piazza XX Septemmbre in Fano, Italy. At Gwinn, she brings the geometric setting to life in much the same way as the putto does the

Fountain terraces, 1957. Photograph by Walter P. Bruning

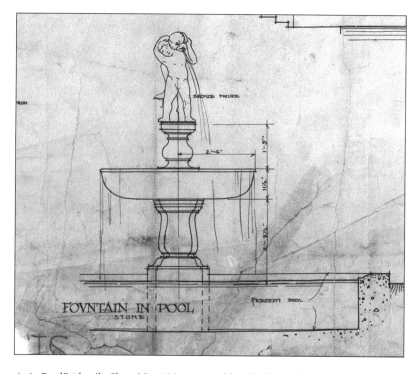

"Fountain in Pool" (detail), Sheet No. 108, prepared by Charles A. Platt, 29 July 1910. Charles Platt Collection, Division of Drawings and Archives, Avery Architectural and Fine Arts Library, Columbia University in the City of New York

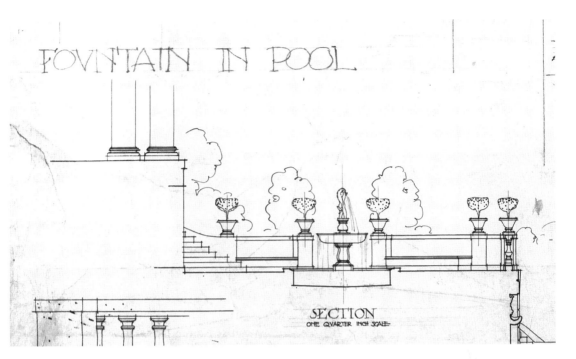

FOVNTAIN IN POOL

SECTION
ONE QVARTER INCH SCALE

"Fountain in Pool" (detail), Sheet No. 108, prepared by Charles A. Platt, 29 July 1910. Charles Platt Collection, Division of Drawings and Archives, Avery Architectural and Fine Arts Library, Columbia University in the City of New York

lake terrace. Platt introduced a larger base and larger, more ornate bowl than the Italian original. He also rerouted the water sprays so that they came from the dolphins' mouths somewhat less effusively than in the original, where artistic license has them spouting from the fishes' nostrils.

Fortuna's first basin, also carved by the Piccirilli Studio, closely resembled that of the dolphin fountain in the wild garden. But mid-decade, Platt and Mather decided that the bowl and supporting base interrupted the view through the central garden axis and substituted a simpler pedestal. Kate Mather had argued in favor of the basin but was overruled.[2]

Ever-vigilant about opportunities for enhancement, Mather wrote Platt in 1912 that a spot near the turn in the drive "looked a little weak and as if it needed some object. I believe one time you suggested a large urn or vase, and I do not want you to forget about this." Two years later, Mather was still reminding Platt of his promise. "I presume you think you are very busy," he teased, "and consequently it may have escaped your mighty mind that you were going to have Mr. Manship prepare under your direction a design for a garden vase."[3]

Paul Manship was a friend of Platt's and a fellow resident of Cornish, where, according to Platt's son, Geoffrey, he often challenged the architect to fierce croquet competitions.[4] After returning in 1912 from a three-year fellowship at the American Academy in Rome, Manship specialized in garden and architectural

Verrochio copy fountain statue and entry to Norway maple allée, after 1912

Wall fountain and terrace, ca. 1913

sculpture. During the 1930s, his work was sought for public spaces. His *Prometheus* for Rockefeller Center, New York City (1934), and the Woodrow Wilson Memorial for the League of Nations in Geneva, Switzerland (1939), were highly praised by critics and remain the sculptor's two best-known public works. Influenced by Greek, Roman, and primitive models, and the geometric rhythms of emerging modernist design, Manship's sculpture emphasized decorative line and crisp modeling. His forms, idealized and untouched by emotion or realism, contrasted with those of American sculptors of the previous generation, including Augustus Saint-Gaudens. Manship's work formalized nature to conform to an abstract idea of beauty, and in that sense it suited Platt's and Mather's taste.

Platt claimed that he had not forgotten the vase project and wrote to tell Mather that Manship was hard at work on a full-size plaster model that would be ready before Mather sailed for Europe in June. Mather must have approved it because the six-foot marble vase was finished the following spring. But once it was installed in its leafy niche, Mather was bothered that he would only be able to see the front of it; half of what Manship had done, half of what he had paid for would remain out of sight. He asked Platt for a revolving platform so he

Formal garden with *Fortuna* and original basin, before 1916

Fortuna without basin, 1957. Photograph by Walter P. Bruning

114

Vase with Great Plains Native Americans by Paul Manship, after 1914

could rotate the piece from time to time. After considerable research, Platt oblig-
ed with a custom-designed turntable.

From a distance, the sculpture program on the vase appeared classical. But a
closer look revealed that the cavorting figures were not the expected nymphs and
satyrs, but Native Americans on horseback. No documents survive to chronicle
the development of the unusual iconography, although the family heard it described as a depiction of Plains Indians hunting pronghorn antelope. Manship's
Remington-style treatment may not have been motivated by a conscious desire
to achieve a "distinctively American" character, but this was certainly its effect.
The spot could have been filled, as similar niches were elsewhere, by a column or
classical figure.

By mid-decade, when most of the new work had been completed, Gwinn's
sculptural program surpassed that of any other Platt garden and figured among
the finest in the country. Rarely was the period's garden statuary so carefully designed or sited. Ubiquitous fauns, satyrs, cherubs, and animals of every description danced, splashed, and hopped their way through hundreds of new American

Manship vase at end of forecourt drive, after 1914

The Muses of Gwinn

landscapes, often plopped down as afterthoughts when an accent was needed to set off a big flower bed or coax a shady nook to life. Many of the new clients, and designers too, were not particularly knowledgeable about sculpture, nor were all budgets swelling at the same rate as Mather's.

At Gwinn, the sculpture did not adhere to a cohesive program, as in the Renaissance tradition, although certain motifs were repeated, the lions, for example, and the dolphins. Nowhere in the surviving correspondence did Platt or Mather express concern about the specific meaning of the figures or their relation to one another. With the possible exception of the Manship vase, the pieces were selected for their visual and emotional appeal—props, essentially, for an elaborate *mise en scène*.

In 1912 Mather asked Platt to design a few architectural changes to the house. The most substantial was a bay window for the morning room at the southeast corner. The room was darker and smaller than many of the others in the house, and the new window would connect the interior more emphatically with the wild garden beyond. For years, Manning had tried to persuade Mather to remove a large oak tree that grew directly in the line of view into the garden and blocked a great deal of light, but Mather liked the tree and refused to have it cut down. It stands there today.

Once the greenhouse was completed and fresh flowers became available year round, Kate Mather asked for a small flower-arranging room. Platt suggested an addition to the morning room at the southeast corner of the house. The tiny room had its own sink, counter, abundant shelf space for vases, and separate entrance. The walls were covered with mirrors so it seemed larger.

Also in 1912 Platt turned his attention to the final element of the amphitheater scheme: the two pavilions for the ends of the sea wall. Unlike the Norway maple allée and the fountains, which were later improvisations, the pavilions had been a part of his plan since its inception. Time as well as financial constraints may have prevented their construction earlier. The design process may also have been unusually slow because Platt was struggling to find the right proportions and materials.

"My idea was to have the columns of stone," he wrote Mather in August, "but . . . I do not feel entirely satisfied that this is the kind of structure required at those places. It seems hardly solid enough for its exposed position, and I am afraid that a more solid building would look too large and not serve any useful purpose, or seem to. I would like a little more time to work out a new scheme for these embellishments. Possibly a more solid column may be used.

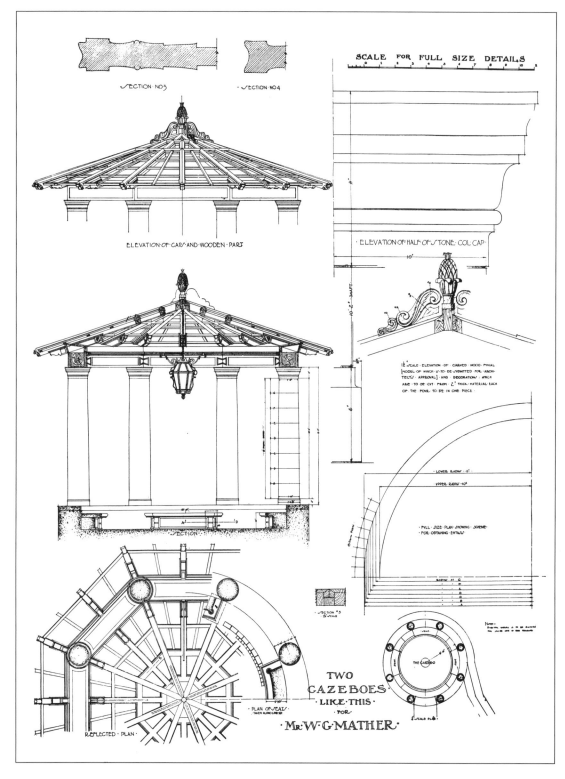

"Two Gazeboes like this for Mr. W. G. Mather," prepared by Charles A. Platt. From Cortissoz, *Monograph of the Work of Charles A. Platt*

View from west gazebo across lake shore, after 1912

I should hesitate about using wood in any case, excepting in the superstructure."[5]

By October, Platt had come up with a new model, which he photographed for Mather. "The scheme, I think, is a good one. The superstructure is to be wood and stained possibly with some color decoration on the inner side of the architrave. The effect of the open work is far better, I think, than any building which had a roof on it, especially in looking down from your portico."[6]

But Mather was unsure about Platt's model, which featured vines draping over the roof. "I doubt if we can rely upon attractive effects from the vines," he warned, "for the severe wind will thresh [sic] them around, and the winter exposure will be very hard." Platt encouraged Mather to come see the models himself in New York and reassured him: "I have had in mind all the time some kind of structure which would look well by itself."[7]

By January, Platt had completed the blueprints for the pavilions and Mather had arranged for a local architect to oversee their construction. (Bohnard and Parsons were also supervising work on a new billiard room on the basement level that opened directly onto the north pool terrace.) The pavilions' lattice roofs with their finely carved pineapple finials may never have gotten the decorative paint Platt initially suggested. However, the silver wood harmonized nicely with the sandstone columns supporting them. Handsome in silhouette, the pavilions permitted views of the water, while their hefty proportions held up admirably to the big lake and the sea wall.

The structures placed visitors out over the lake in a psychologically separate space from the green garden. The wave-whipped platforms offered an exhilarating perspective. The complexity and emotional impact of Gwinn's landscape were expanding with time.

CHAPTER ELEVEN

THE BIG WILD GARDEN

IN 1912 MATHER purchased twenty-one additional acres south of Lake Shore Boulevard with an eye to developing much of it into "a species of wild garden" like those Manning was designing for other clients. Mather wrote to Manning to explain that he wanted the new garden "made available in the best way by paths, encouragement of the native growth, and planting of additional interesting growth" and asked him to advise on the project. Manning was undoubtedly pleased, especially since the first wild garden had recently been so thoroughly Italianized. He was confident that the woods would suit Mather, whom he later described as one "who must have a home near the city and who wants with it some of the infinite beauty and variety of wilderness, wildlife in woodland and stream, and with the sparkling ripple of rapids and the quiet pools that mirror the beauty of sky, clouds, trees and flowers."[1]

By January 1913, a month after receiving Mather's first letter about the project, Manning had already finished a preliminary plan for the new garden, mapping out a system of trails through the existing woods. The plan took its cues from the twisting course of Nine Mile Creek as it ran through the rough and hilly terrain. "It was difficult to believe that the stream was not flowing backward in places," wrote Manning, "as I encountered one crook after another in passing through the woods." The unpredictable creek created havoc by fre-

"Gwinn" (detail showing wild garden), Plan No. 935-59-2, prepared by Warren H. Manning Offices, Inc., 13 January 1931

quently overrunning its banks, but Manning wrote, "we must give this stream credit for carving out a picturesque and varied lay of the land with high and low bluff, broad and narrow ridges and swales, and for laying down rich soils." Manning was particularly excited about the large variety of plants they would be able to grow on the site and later recorded their names in extensive notes.[2]

Before setting down a final plan, Manning commissioned a local man, E. E. Boalt, to survey the land. In addition to whatever buildings were missing from his own earlier survey, he asked for elevations, contours, and "local incidents," including "steep slopes, gradual slopes, small gulleys, water courses, glades, locations of important trees, and masses of shrubbery."[3] The new land would be Manning's canvas; before beginning his composition he wanted to know all its subtleties.

In response to the detailed information, Manning set about laying out a plan that would offer the greatest possible variety of woodland experiences based on a path system of maximum interest and length. Eventually, the curving network of winding foot and horse trails crisscrossed the stream with six bridges, one of which was designed by Platt.[4] In 1920 Platt also created a summerhouse for one of the eminences in the woods. A wooden viewing platform was constructed for another hill; several flights of stairs linked trails and paths.

After receiving Manning's preliminary plan in January 1913, Mather quickly sent a copy to Platt for his review. But Platt seemed more interested in a porcelain collection he and Mather were about to visit than the new project. At the end of a letter, he wrote simply, "It looks all right so far as I can judge on paper. It gives an interesting development of the woods."[5] That was enough for Mather.

Poised to leave on a four-month trip to Europe, Mather authorized Manning to spend from six to eight thousand dollars creating the wild garden that spring. It was not a trivial sum, yet Mather was spending several times that amount on single works of art for his collection. Given his experience with the first garden, he may have figured that the investment would be repeated. Despite the circumscribed budget, Manning took the project seriously. He wrote to Charles Heer, Mather's secretary, that he did not even "intend to expend the full amount" and also guaranteed, "this is a matter that I intend to give enough of my personal attention, so that I may be assured of satisfactory results."[6]

Manning came out to Cleveland in early February to walk the land with Jacques and take detailed notes. With the new data collected, he refined his preliminary plan and began to create plant lists. He asked Jacques about the possibility of propagating certain varieties from root and top cuttings in order to keep costs down. Among the plants he recommended were "Monarda didyma coccinea, Asters in any variety, Boltonias in any variety, Helenium in any variety, Helianthus, Chelone, or any similar native plant of which you have a stock on the ground."[7] Although this first written record of plants for the new area specified native varieties, Manning did not mean to restrict his focus. Later letters suggest that he was primarily interested in robustness and richness of effect; native plants would have been by definition generally well suited to the task, and so several were included from the start.

Another of Manning's early, although unspoken, goals was to create a strong working alliance with Jacques. Particularly after his experiences with the first wild garden, Manning realized how heavily the success of the new venture depended on Jacques's interest in it. In his February letter he asked the gardener's advice about which annuals they might try to introduce on the clay field slopes.

Manning also asked Jacques to spade out most of the "uninteresting" herbaceous material on the ground, but leave "all tree seedlings as well as Sumachs

Pavilion in wild garden designed by Platt, 1920, photograph ca. 1930

Field Edge Path, wild garden, ca. 1930

and other shrubs," and try "varieties like Petunia, Bachelor's Button, Caliopsis, Cleome pungens" and poppies.[8] The boldness of these blooms suggests that the pictures forming in Manning's imagination were ones of broad sheets of color.

Jacques proved more enthusiastic than Manning could have dared hope. In mid-February, he began laying out trails. Heer wrote to alert Manning of the speed with which the project was unfolding. By this time Mather was in Europe, so it was left to the three men—Manning, Heer, and the impatient Jacques—to coordinate their efforts independently of their boss.

Manning was alarmed, too, and wrote Heer that although "Jacques undoubtedly has a general idea as to the location of trails through the woods, I do not want him to go ahead with these without indicating on a sketch to me where he is placing them and where he proposes to place them, because I have pretty definite ideas as to the detailed treatment which I want to carry out…. Can't you arrange at once to have him send me a sketch on the accompanying print of the

Clearing edged with rhododendron, wild garden, ca. 1930

paths that he has already laid down, and those that he proposes to lay down, so
that I can pass upon them and include them in my study?"[9]

Manning reviewed Jacques's efforts and found them to be sound. By late
February the new project was once again proceeding with harmony and ever-ac-
celerating enthusiasm on Jacques's part. The new wild garden seems to have captured his imagination as the formal garden never did. A work force of forty men,
overseen by Jacques and E. J. Cotter, Manning's superviser from Ishpeming,
cleared and planted the new garden in about three months. By May 1913, the
larger share of the grading, planting, and building had been completed. Manning
later told Mather that he thought Jacques and Cotter had performed a "miracle"
in accomplishing so much so well and so quickly.[10]

The quantities and varieties of plants used in the new garden were extraordinary. Sixteen boxcar loads of five hundred rhododendrons each were dug in
Damascus, Virginia, and planted the first year. Four hundred sacks of peat, also
from Virginia, were sent to enrich the stiff soil. In addition to rosebay, Carolina,

and catawba rhododendrons, the cars also contained mountain laurel and thousands of square feet of heart leaf wild ginger, Canada wild ginger, and American maidenhair fern.

The first year, Jacques propagated five thousand plants from Gwinn's flower and vegetable gardens, including two thousand Oswego beebalm that were planted in a hundred-foot swale near the woods' Sunflower Path. Sunflower *Heliopsis* and red sneezewort were planted in great quantities. Thousands of Japanese honeysuckle, Grecian silk vine, and cutleaf blackberry were set out along the stream banks. Cotter sent down three thousand blue marsh violets from Ishpeming.

Spring flowering bulbs were ordered from Holland in lots of one to five thousand for fall planting. Manning's list included lily leek, Siberian squills, Spanish squills, common star-of-Bethlehem, common snowdrop, poet's *Narcissus*, *Crocus*, common grape hyacinth, white grape hyacinth, and tiger lily. Five hundred plants each of crested iris and Crimean iris in variety were planted. One

Field edged with *Hemerocallis fulva*, wild garden, ca. 1930

Fern Glade Path, wild garden, ca. 1930

thousand shooting-star came from Wisconsin. Tawny daylily and iris in variety were planted along the easterly side of Field Edge path. Eventually each trail, bridge, glade, set of steps, and even major tree (King Elm, King Cotton, King Maple) was named. The path names read like a Whitmanesque chant: Pawpaw, Hemlock, Rosebay, Water Leaf, Stag Horn, Bluff Top, Bittersweet, Primrose, Field Edge, Spicewood, Wood Thrush, Blue Bells, Ginger Root, Bamboo.

In spring 1914 five hundred butterfly weed were brought from New Jersey. Climbing hempweed was planted along some of the stream banks where silk vine and blackberry had failed. Ginseng, spikenard, great Solomon's-seal, small Solomon's-seal, *Mertensia*, and false Solomon's-seal were added. Violets were set out along the walk on the top of the bank among arborvitae; thousands of tawny daylily were planted on the slope. Double tansy was brought in quantity from North Carolina. Walking fern (*Camptosorus rhizophyllus*), imported from Virginia, and Hart's-tongue were also planted in quantity.

More American spikenard came from Illinois the following spring. At that time American ginseng, also from Illinois, was planted on the slope near the

Jewell Walk. Three species of leeks went in with native allium along the Ridge Path. Mock cucumber (*Echinocystia lobata*) was put along the stream with more climbing hempweed (*Mikania scandens*). Orange groundsel was planted from seed received from Cyrus H. McCormick, whose Lake Forest estate, Walden, was undergoing similar development.

Jacques planted joe-pye weed and other thoroughworts in the open clay soil. Groundsel bush, aster, marshmallows, and about one dozen varieties of goldenrod were introduced. Manning donated spike speedwell from his family home in Billerica, Massachusetts.

On the stream's western bank, Carolina poplar, graceful sunflower, giant sunflower, prairie coneflower, musk mallow, showy coneflower, and several other hardy sunflowers were planted. Cutleaf grapefern and adder's-tongue fern were added in abundance.

The success of Manning's design depended on his creating impressive drifts of single varieties. In later writing he criticized the widespread "tendency . . . to make a mixed-up jumble of many kinds of plants to gain variety or to find a place for

Bog, wild garden, ca. 1930

Field Edge Path with *Knifophia uvaria*, ca. 1930

Bridge in wild garden, ca. 1930

new kinds that friends may suggest and the salesman urge you to buy. It is better to have great masses of floral color and of foliage, fruit, and twig values so arranged as to give effective displays of color, form, and texture for each period of the year."[11]

Despite Manning's expertise, not everything took hold. Each year new species were tried in the wild garden. Some thrived, some disappeared quickly. To Manning, arguably the country's most knowledgeable plantsman, it was one grand experiment—the failures were as interesting as the successes. He kept track of it all, viewing the wild garden as a prototype for other clients. "The ideal estates of the future," Manning wrote late in life, "will be large, wild land areas with much variation in surface conditions—hills with far-reaching views—valleys—streams—ponds—the great lakes and the sea—and much forest area.... The owner's pleasure will come from opening wood roads, bridle paths, and foot paths ... and in opening vistas and views ... of notable trees, shrubs, and ground covers on the property and in the distance."[12]

Vista from Gwinn's lawn, looking across Lake Shore Boulevard, after 1912

By the end of the first year, Manning felt satisfied with what had been accomplished. "I took the time to run through the wild garden late yesterday afternoon," he wrote to Mather on 8 May 1914. "The white grape hyacinths, the violets and the bluebells, especially, were fine. Evidently the wild garden is going to be a success for, as I saw it, it came up to my expectations."

But the garden was far from finished. After his spring visit to Cleveland the following year, Manning was "much impressed with the need of a more effective overhead floral display." He suggested adding flowering trees such as dogwood, redbud, and others that would grow successfully at the edge of openings in the woods, along the streams, and in open fields. For this purpose, he also recommended apples, crabapples, peaches, apricots, *Koelreuteria* (golden rain tree), and pink hawthorn. "We already have Chinese Wistarias planted at the base of certain trees in the woods," he wrote Mather, "up which they will climb to give flowers after a time, but this result will not come until quite a number of years. However, early results can be secured with the trees I am speaking of." Many other experiments would follow.[13]

It was Mather's own idea, after his 1912 European trip, to unite the home grounds and new wild garden visually with a long, almost nine-hundred-foot, Lombardy poplar allée. The double row of trees stretched from the south side of Lake Shore Boulevard to the Field Edge path, which marked the eastern boundary of the new wild garden. At Platt's suggestion the poplars were planted to follow the line of elms on Gwinn's front lawn. The trees grew quickly and, once the rhododendrons had filled in to cover the open grillwork in the boulevard fence, they offered the illusion of great land holdings, as well as a memorable view from the south porch. As improvements at Gwinn went, the allée was one of the more economical: at the time, eighteen-foot Lombardy poplars (then known as *Populus fastigiata*) sold for seventy cents apiece.

Still, there was no easy answer to the problem of how to connect the physical circulation of the new piece of land with the old when a busy street divided the two. Mather's idea was to extend the long west garden walk, which began in Gwinn's forecourt and ran the length of the formal and cutting gardens. The path would cross the boulevard and continue to the boundary land belonging to Mather's neighbor, H. G. Dalton—a total of more than 750 feet. "At this point," Mather wrote, "a jog is required ... we turn at right angles to the right and enter the winding walks of the wild garden."[14]

Despite Mather's pleas to buy the land and so dispense with the awkward detour, his neighbor absolutely refused to sell. Ironically, the parcel had, only a short time before, belonged to Mather. Mather confided to Platt that in selling the land, he was afraid he had "parted with his birthright."[15]

"If I were going to give you real Italian advice of the 15th Century," Platt wrote jovially, "I should advise adopting the line indicated in bluepencil which goes bang, straight, to the wild garden. [But] this would probably involve war with Mr. Dalton."[16] Mather opted for the less confrontational solution of a jog in the path.

In 1934 a local horticulturist named Paul Young and his wife came to live in Gwinn's then-vacant farmhouse in exchange for raising fruits, vegetables, and poultry for the household. Young later remembered his years there with fondness and excitement. The wild garden seemed "a fairyland," reported Young, whose otherwise vivid memories did not extend to the name of the man who designed the woodland: "It had been laid out by Frederick Law Olmsted," he wrote, "the famous landscape architect from Boston. He had planted thousands of daffodils and scillas around the edge of the woods and those were all in bloom. And the scillas, there were just sheets of blue ... just like a piece of the sky falling down. And the daffodils were yellow,... and everything in bloom—my gosh, we thought, this is just heaven!"[17]

The new woods could not have contrasted more vividly with the home grounds across the street. From the first stirrings of spring, the wild garden was alive with sweeps of color. The movement of the seasons was marked by new blooms, new birdsong, and new scents rising from the woodland floor. Manning's design was structured by a path system determined by the earth itself.

Mather grew to love his new garden, perhaps even preferring it, as Manning had foreseen, to the geometric elegance of the home grounds.[18] As the years advanced, he spent many contented hours there on foot and on horseback, exploring its changing mysteries.

CHAPTER TWELVE

THE MIDDLE YEARS

MATHER'S QUEST to improve Gwinn continued through the decade. In January 1914, he wrote Platt: "My formal garden did not look as well last year as it should.... The colors that were in it last year were a little too startling, I think, owing to Jacques having used a great deal of red geraniums and at certain times of the year it did not have sufficient bloom. You doubtless have some person whom you use to make planting plans for such gardens, and I should be glad to have your suggestions in the matter." Mather enclosed a list of the plants Jacques was in the habit of using. Platt, in turn, sent the list and a copy of the plan to his friend and colleague Ellen Shipman. He had told Mather that Mrs. Shipman would "probably want, after she has studied the thing, to come out and see the garden, and probably talk to you on the spot, but I have asked her to criticize the plan, and make some suggestions for its improvement beforehand."[1]

Ellen Shipman made her first visit to Gwinn in April that year. Her suggestions apparently met with Mather's approval, for she was given jurisdiction over plantings in the four sections of the formal garden surrounding the central pool. Her plans are lost, but correspondence details her recommendation of at least five new plants: pink, lavender, and white stock, *Phlox Drummondii*, and marigolds. Undoubtedly, the complete list would have been much longer; her plans typically included hundreds of varieties of perennials and annuals.

In general, the new planting design respected the garden's original lines. But one set of instructions to Jacques concerning the placement of plants within the

Formal garden, before 1935

beds indicates an interesting departure from Platt's approach: "Well defined lines of demarcation are to be avoided," she advised, "except that the borders themselves will, of course, be straight and parallel with the walk."[2] According to Platt's original plan, a strict geometry dictated placement so that the plants were essentially put down in rows. Shipman's design called for drifts of plants, a technique that recalled the work of Gertrude Jekyll, whose gardens Ellen Shipman would have known well.

Three weeks later, however, a problem arose between Shipman and Jacques. She had assumed that Jacques would implement her design plan precisely, but his assumption apparently differed. "I regret extremely," she wrote Mather, "there should have been any misunderstanding as to what I am to do. I thought when I left Gwinn and again on receiving your first letter that everything was perfectly clear."[3] Apparently Shipman's role as adviser to Jacques had never been clarified.

"I gather from your telegram," she continued exasperatedly, "that you now wish to go by Jacques's instructions on the papers enclosed in our letter rather than on the plan agreed upon." Besides changing the plantings on the ground,

Jacques had apparently edited some of her suggestions out of the seed order, including the pink, lavender, and white stock. Shipman informed Mather that she had superseded Jacques's order and sent for these herself.

With the entire estate within his purview, Jacques had long before developed his own priorities; the formal garden, already one of the most maintenance-intensive features at Gwinn, does not appear to have been high on his list. Under his care, its plantings had changed substantially since its inception in 1908. All that remained from the original supply of annuals, according to Shipman's letter, were "heliotrope, geraniums and snapdragons," the latter having gained considerable territory throughout the garden. ("I thought it best," Shipman wrote, "to eliminate all the snapdragons from the beds you wished me to do.")[4] Shipman's characteristically subtle and complex planting plans may not have impressed Jacques as much of an improvement. Or they may have seemed to represent an exceedingly demanding project—one for which he had neither the time nor the interest.

But in June, after Shipman's second visit, Mather sent her a conciliatory note, pledging "assiduous attention to your bed." He added, "Jacques has assured me that he will also give careful supervision to it so that it may have every opportunity of developing as you desire." He feared that because he would be in Europe over the summer, he would "not be able to enjoy the fruition" of Shipman's plan, but noted that his sister would "remain at home and will get all the benefit of it."[5] No photographs survive to show whether the new plan became a regular feature, but it probably did not. In 1925 "too glamorous masses of the yellow Celosia" (cockscomb—not a plant Shipman would likely have suggested) attracted the attention of the local press.[6] In any case, Ellen Shipman did not return to Gwinn until the 1930s.

The First World War curtailed Warren Manning's practice and completely shut down Platt's office. Prospective homebuilders were not so apt to undertake ambitious new residences and gardens during uncertain times. Shortages of labor and materials as well as burgeoning patriotic feelings—a widespread sense that personal comforts were not to be indulged at prewar intensities—discouraged the sorts of projects in which Platt specialized. His work for Mather during the period was also minimal.

Gwinn played its own small role in the war drama. In 1917 a group of wealthy Cleveland residents decided to raise money for a European children's relief fund by creating a full length film and donating all proceeds from its showings. In *Perils of Society* the amateur cast (which did not include William

Marble planter in drive, 1993. Photograph by Carol Betsch

Mather) spoofed their luxurious, admittedly self-indulgent lives with scenes at the racetrack, sports club, local restaurants, and Cleveland's estates, including Gwinn. The film was part Marx Brothers and part *cinema verité*, both satire and self-confessional exposé. Scenes from Gwinn's landscape appeared throughout the film: the north portico with the recently planted Norway maple allée, the fountain-splashed forecourt, the formal garden, and the newly formalized wild garden provided evocative stage sets throughout. The closing scene of the movie showed the film's star-crossed lovers embracing on the fountain terrace, silhouetted against the sunset.

After the war and throughout the 1920s, Warren Manning continued to make yearly visits to Gwinn, advising on seasonal planting and maintenance. He focused most of his attention on developing the new wild garden and repairing damage done by the annually flooding creek. In 1920 Mather hired Manning for landscape work around several new Michigan mines, including the Mackinaw and the Gwinn. Manning's other Upper Peninsula projects for Mather included high schools, cemeteries, residential grounds, clubhouses, dams, and railroad yards. In Munising, he planned a town extension and low-cost housing, the school, the hospital, the Beech Inn, and, on Grand Island (which Mather owned), a summer camp colony.

George Jacques's death in 1923 was a blow to both Mather and Manning. Over the years Jacques had accumulated a demanding roster of duties, including directing a staff of about a dozen workers. As a superintendent he had matured gracefully, even brilliantly. Prospects of finding an equally able successor seemed dismal until Manning hit upon the idea of offering the job to Jacques's daughter, Lillie, who had grown up at Gwinn and often helped her father in his work there. Mather liked the idea and readily agreed. Lillie accepted.

According to one newspaper account, Lillie Jacques was the only woman estate superintendent in the world and the only female member of the American Gardeners' Association. "Inheriting a love for garden management from her grandfather and father," the article related, "Miss Jacques, 'just grew into the work.' . . . Beginning as a foreman, under her father, . . . she gained her practical and technical knowledge [from] him." The untraditional arrangement seemed to work well. By 1927 news spread of Lillie Jacques's prize-winning chrysanthemums and her work training peach trees on trellises (one of these, she explained, was to be a centerpiece for the dinner table as "Mr. Mather likes to pick his dinner fruits from the tree").[7] Continuing her work as superintendent after her marriage in the early 1930s, Lillie Jacques Mook assumed her father's deep involvement with the wild garden and worked closely with Manning and the Mathers until mid-decade. The circumstances of her departure from Gwinn are not known.

Mather and Platt remained in touch even though there was little architectural work at Gwinn again until later in the decade. Occasional shooting parties, bridge weekends, and visits in New York City offered both men respite from busy work schedules. Platt made his first trip "up the lakes" with Mather in 1912. It was a luxurious event, a treat for many of Mather's friends and business colleagues, particularly after the construction of the new *William G. Mather* in 1925.

One of six Great Lakes bulk carriers commissioned at the time—the first two were for the Ford Motor Company—the 618-foot, fifteen-thousand-ton-capacity *William G. Mather* was one of the two largest ships on the lakes. The ship was recognizable at a distance by its distinctive colors; Platt, true to his role as Mather's chief aesthetic adviser, helped select the unusual shade of olive green for the pilot house—unique among the vessels of the day. A red "C" on the rear smokestack identified the vessel as the flagship of the fleet.

In the oak-paneled guest dining room, Mather and his party supped from crystal and china marked with the C.C.I. insignia. They ate well. Because food was all-important to crew morale, Great Lakes shipping companies competed ferociously for talented cooks. Cleveland-Cliffs was in a position to hire the best. Invited guests included clients, potential clients, executives, politicians, employees, and Mather's new bride. There is no record of Warren Manning's making the trip to upper Michigan aboard the *William G. Mather*, although his work often took him there.[8]

Elizabeth Ring Ireland, widow of James Ireland, Mather's friendly competitor in the iron-ore business, had lived next door to Gwinn with her only son for many years. Her house enjoyed a similar prospect and shared a garden wall along Gwinn's service drive. By coincidence, Elizabeth Ireland was also an acquaintance of Charles Platt, having spent part of her childhood in a house Platt designed for her parents in 1903–4, in Saginaw, Michigan.

In October 1927 Mather wrote Platt about a conversation he had just had "with our mutual friend, Mrs. Ireland" regarding a new gateway they wanted to have built into the wall that separated the two estates—ostensibly to make things easier for the postman. "We have finally decided to impose upon your good nature and ask for your advice," Mather wrote, "accompanied by a sketch and sufficient specifications to enable us to put the thing in process of erection by workmen here."[9] Platt supplied the desired design with a casual sketch. He probably knew that the gate symbolized more than a simple convenience: visits between the two households were becoming increasingly frequent.

Sketch of gate by Charles Platt, 1929

The *William G. Mather*, 18 May 1929

Consequently, Platt may have been one of the very few people who were not surprised when, two years later, Elizabeth, age thirty-eight, and William, age seventy-one, were married at Cleveland's Trinity Episcopal Cathedral. After the ceremony, the couple quietly boarded the *William G. Mather* and vanished on an upper Michigan honeymoon. Cleveland's high society had been caught offguard; not a word had leaked beyond the family before the event took place, and apparently not even all the family were alerted. According to local memory, Elizabeth sent a telegram to her elderly uncle inviting him to the church ceremony but not telling him what the occasion was. Assuming he was invited to a memorial service for Elizabeth's first husband, the uncle sent a funeral wreath. William proved a good sport: "Just cut it in half," he told Elizabeth, "and put one half around each of our necks."[10]

After Elizabeth and William's marriage, Kate moved next door into Elizabeth's old house before moving permanently to Cooperstown, New York. She continued to winter in Pasadena, California, where William also had a home.

Like William, Elizabeth was an active member of many of Cleveland's charitable, religious, and educational boards. She was also a prominent member and president of the Garden Club of Cleveland, the chair of the central zone of the

Elizabeth Ring Mather on fountain terrace, after 1929

Garden Club of America, and the first president of the Garden Center of Greater Cleveland. Elizabeth served on the board of trustees of Rainbow Children's Hospital, the Visiting Nurses Association, the Family Service Association, the Holden Arboretum, and the Saginaw Museum of Art, and was an advisory committee member of the Cleveland Museum of Art. She was competent, articulate, and strong-willed.

Platt's architectural services were called upon again when Elizabeth moved into what her husband had been in the habit of calling "Platt's room" at Gwinn, the bedroom in the northwest corner of the house. She decided to redecorate both it and William's room—enlarging closets, creating modern, more luxurious baths, and making the Italian decor more pronounced with new furniture, rugs, and ceiling paintings. She also proposed finishing the interior of the still-unused third floor, suggesting that a modernistic mural be added to stairway, "suggestive of sky effects, with some gulls and airplanes mounting along with the steps." Platt was in the process of helping Elizabeth find an artist for the wall painting when the stock market crashed.[11] Mather's personal finances were not irrevocably affected, but a new sense of fiscal restraint quickly emerged. The third-floor decoration was one of the first casualties.

As discussion about the bedroom renovations evolved, it seemed that Elizabeth might challenge Platt's design authority. But William defended his architect's role as final arbiter of taste at Gwinn. "As I said when we were last together," Mather wrote Platt, "I am relying on you to shape up these changes which my wife wants so that they will be satisfactory to you as well as to her."[12] Although Platt's distinctive eye regulated major changes at Gwinn, the house furnishings were not a static collection. When new furniture came to Gwinn from the Ring house in Saginaw, Michigan—admittedly a Platt design—the pieces fit in agreeably.

Despite Elizabeth's enthusiasm, William was not particularly keen about changes to his private rooms. He confided to Platt, "I am not very much interested in having them Italianized to the extent that appeals to [Elizabeth]."[13] But two weeks later Mather relented and wrote, somewhat resignedly, "Elizabeth seems to wish my room to be in a similar style to hers."[14] Platt's quotes fell within the Mathers' budget, and the renovations were carried out. Several new artworks were added, including a Della Robbia relief (from the Ireland house), new rugs were woven, and the bathrooms assumed a new marbleized elegance.[1]

Elizabeth's bedroom after renovation, after 1929

Garden party at Gwinn, after 1935

Cottonwood Vista in autumn, wild garden, ca. 1930

CHAPTER THIRTEEN

THE DEPRESSION
YEARS

MANNING AND MATHER'S friendship deepened during the Depression. "I will surely stop to see you, who are among my dearest and oldest friends, whenever I can," Manning wrote in November 1933. Two years later he recollected "the joys of our intercourse of the past third of a century that has been so much of an inspiration to me."[1] One of the subjects of their meetings during the period was how best to keep Gwinn in shape as resources steadily shrank.

Early in the decade, Manning told Mather that he wanted to write a history of Gwinn's landscape for publication. He envisioned a narrative text, photographs ("to illustrate the plant materials that are dominant factors in the pictorial values"), and appendixes with plant lists and data about their performance. Manning said he wanted the volume to include "as complete a concise history of the plants and their behavior from the beginning as is practicable." He mentioned other publications as models, a book titled *Landscape Art* prepared for Cyrus McCormick about his estate, Walden, and the 1913 Platt monograph with a foreword by Royal Cortissoz, which featured Mather's estate along with several others.[2]

Mather agreed to subsidize the cost of photographs taken under Manning's direction by A. D. Taylor, A. G. Eldredge, and Manning's son, J. Woodward Manning. The otherworldly images show the large wild garden at its peak—

Amphitheatre Bridge and Carolina Steps, wild garden, ca. 1930

when the plantings were well established but maintenance had not yet been reduced. Mather also agreed to underwrite the time it took Manning to compile
the long plant lists and work with Lillie Jacques Mook in documenting the complete trail system of the wild garden. Together Lillie Mook, Elizabeth Mather,
and Manning named the trails in preparation for the book.

Manning may have been motivated to write Gwinn's history by the desire to
document his landscape oeuvre. Around the same time, he also wrote a long autobiography but was unable to organize the vast amount of material into read-
able form and the manuscript was never published.[3] But Manning also believed
that Gwinn could be a useful prototype for other residential landscapes; in 1930
he could scarcely have foreseen how rare such projects would become.

A lack of much else to do with his time made the writing projects possible.
The field of landscape architecture had changed dramatically since Manning had
opened his practice nearly fifty years earlier. He was seventy when the stock
market crashed and was accustomed to running a large office with a big staff.

Masses of *Rhododendron maximum* and *carolinianum*, wild garden, ca. 1930

But each year brought fewer clients, and he was forced to curtail his operation. One of Manning's specific areas of expertise—planting design—was suffering a dramatic devaluation, and another of his strong interests—planning—had been paralyzed by the economic crisis. Opportunities to teach, lecture, write, and consult, which often arise at the end of a successful career, did not fall to Manning, or to many of his colleagues.

Although he was never entirely enthusiastic about the Gwinn publication, Mather did seem willing to pursue at least the initial stage. By August 1930 Manning had finished a first draft and sent it to Mather for his "very frank criticisms." He told Mather that he wanted to write one more section, tentatively titled "Lessons of Gwinn" or "What We Have Learned from Gwinn," but neither it nor Mather's personal recollections, which Manning also requested, were ever added to the text. Mather apparently did review the manuscript and offer suggestions, as a second, more concise version of the Gwinn narrative exists.[4]

The following year, a copy of Manning's revised draft was sent to a university press (which one is not known), but the publication plan seems to have involved a large subsidy from Mather. He wrote to Manning that he felt unsure about continuing: "The expenditures seem considerable as well as the size of the book."[5] A final decision not to publish was made sometime later in 1931, a reflection, surely, of the Mathers' steadily worsening financial situation. The project was not mentioned again, at least in the correspondence.

Manning's thirty-two-page narrative and the photographs taken for it were eventually mounted into a Mather family scrapbook. Manning's ingenuous writing style captures his heartfelt enthusiasm for Gwinn. The first paragraph opens with the fundamental premise that guided the estate's development from the beginning: "Gwinn is a dream of a home-maker realized, wherein all forms of beauty in Art or Nature are conserved, created, associated, and harmonized in ways that give pleasure to all observers." Manning's practical side was also in evidence as he noted that the project had been undertaken "without evidence of extravagance in costs or in upkeep."

In 1932 Manning approached Mather with another project: opening the woods south of the boulevard to the public. Manning had convinced many of his clients, including Frank Seiberling, to buy, develop, and donate land for public enjoyment. But Mather was hesitant; his situation was different from Seiberling's. Stan Hywet encompassed hundreds of acres of land and merged easily into what would become Akron's Metropolitan Park System, much of which had been donated by Seiberling's neighbors, at Manning's and Seiberling's

Cottonwood Vista, wild garden, ca. 1930

Rhododendron glade, wild garden, ca. 1930

encouragement. Because Gwinn's setting was suburban and surrounded by other homes, problems of parking, circulation, and public use were more difficult to solve, particularly since the Mathers still wanted to occupy their house.

William Mather responded to Manning's idea with guarded interest: "[Your] suggestions with regard to Gwinn seem radical to us who have been living on the North side of the Boulevard with a feeling that we could walk over to the South side and enjoy a private walk in the seclusion of the verdant forest which you have done so much to beautify, but perhaps we are selfish, and perhaps, further, we cannot afford any more to be selfish in that respect." He concluded on a positive note. "The next time you come out we will have a talk in regard to the matter."[6] Although no decisions were made at the time, Manning's notion of Gwinn's broadened role foreshadowed the estate's eventual use and may in fact have been the germinal idea for the Mathers' later establishment of a fund to ensure Gwinn's survival.

In 1934 Manning sent Mather yet another proposal, this one for developing a master plan—"concerning house, education, recreation, and subsistence gardens and field plots"—for the several upper Michigan communities associated with Cleveland-Cliffs. "There is so little work in my office now," Manning wrote, "that I could give all my time to it."[7] Mather responded that he was "bearing [the] suggestion in mind," but he did not commission Manning for the project.[8]

A month later, Manning wrote again to his friend about the hard times: "You will see that I and in fact, most of the people in my profession, as well as in the Architects' profession are in the same boat.... I am fortunate in having an insurance annuity that will keep me going personally, but not my office." He continued, "You will I am sure realize that it is a relief to open up one's vial of woes to a dear old friend, as you did to some extent to me when I was last there. I keep busy, however, every minute, eat well, sleep well and refuse to be discouraged."[9]

While Manning was working to record Gwinn for posterity, he was watching aspects of its design slip away. Mather wrote in spring of 1933 to ask his advice in "keeping the garden in as nice a shape as possible." Two weeks later, he confided to Platt that "owing to the depression" he had decided to maintain only the "Italian Garden and the lawns and [keep] visitors away from all other parts of the place."[10] Manning recommended that some of the formal garden panels be turfed over, regular pruning and replanting be suspended, and, what may have been most difficult for him personally, all maintenance in the big wild garden be stopped. He also suggested that Mather stop manicuring the front lawn.

But this last struck Mather as imprudent. A well-groomed front lawn seemed important to the overall impression of Gwinn. "I can imagine this area," Mather argued, "if it had flowers domesticated in the grass, as we have at Cliffs Cottage along the hillsides... but would it be a success in the formal surroundings of Gwinn?"[11]

"What I had in mind especially," Manning teased, "was [to eliminate] that flock of bipeds without feathers and in dresses that I have seen creeping over the lawn in search of 'weeds.' [Every summer Mather hired groups of Italian women to hand weed the lawn.] Some of these weeds do have an interest and beauty.... Encourage the creepers, especially the nearly evergreen ones, such as the Speedwells or Veronicas, Bugle, Creeping Dandelion, English Daisy, with Moneywort and Creeping Jenny all of which can be walked on comfortably.... Then keep a limited area near the terrace in perfect grass and let it run into the ground creepers."[12] Mather adopted a modified version of Manning's plan but never completely let go of the idea of a proper front lawn.

The 1930s brought many losses to Mather, both financial and personal. With his private fortune greatly reduced, he decided to sell the personal library he had amassed over the decades. Mather's dedication to the collection had been extraordinary; under his sponsorship several bibliographies had been prepared by a private librarian. The decision to sell, particularly at a time when the market was so poor, was, no doubt, an agonizing one. In 1931 William's brother, Samuel, died; eight years later, in 1939, Kate died. This surely must have seemed the end of an era.

Charles Platt's practice fell off sharply as the Depression wore on. Only a few new projects, mainly for institutions, came into the office during the early 1930s; among the most significant were a campus plan for Deerfield Academy, an infirmary and chapel for Phillips Academy, and a new president's house at the University of Illinois at Urbana. On 1 January 1933, when Platt announced a new partnership with his two sons, Geoffrey and William, there was no work in the office at all.

Eight months later, Platt died at the age of seventy-two. He had never enjoyed particularly robust health, and his final years had been marked by decreasing stamina. The last years of Platt's practice were a muted close to what had been a brilliant career. Architecture, like landscape architecture, had changed enormously since he had begun practicing four decades earlier. Platt, and most of his architectural colleagues, had been caught by a dramatic reversal of circumstances, both financial and aesthetic. The market for country houses shrank steadily, and many of the best of them deteriorated as the resources to keep

Warren Manning, Lillie Jacques Mook, and unidentified man sitting on overlook platform, wild garden, ca. 1930

them in good shape disappeared.

The grand landscapes of the period were even more vulnerable than the houses to the natural forces of entropy. Most of Manning's sizable residential designs were hard hit during the final years of the Depression. Certain clients, like Mather, were able to maintain the core of their properties, but a great number were not.

Many of the changes in the profession that had been precipitated by the stock market crash proved permanent, presaging dramatic cultural and social upheavals and shifts in life styles and values. The boom time for estate gardens was almost over. The entry of the United States into World War II at the end of 1941 would finish off the Country Place Era. The artistic legacies of Platt, Manning, and hundreds of their colleagues were quickly obscured by changing tastes and fortunes.

CHAPTER FOURTEEN

RENEWAL

BY 1935 THE MATHERS' finances had sufficiently improved for them to begin thinking about restoring Gwinn to a modest version of its former glory. The staff was doubled to four men (Lillie Mook had left by then), Manning was invited to return to advise, and Ellen Shipman was hired once again to design a planting scheme for the formal garden—it had been twenty-one years since she had last worked at Gwinn.

Concerns about maintenance do not seem to have subdued Shipman's imagination as she drafted the planting plan that reached the Mathers in September. The plan respected the basic configurations determined by Charles Platt in 1908, but involved changing most of the plants and buying about four thousand new ones. Her design called for matching pairs of beds with some subtle differences between them to accommodate collections of showier varieties such as Japanese iris, peonies, and lilies.[1]

Two sets of four small beds that sat in front of the teahouse and the pergola were designed in east-west pairs; the four rectangular beds bordering the grass panels and pool corresponded diagonally. Platt's color scheme of blue, white, and yellow was preserved but softened with pale pinks and apricots. Platt's signature bay trees were kept, as were most of the barberry hedges bordering the beds. The new plan reflected Shipman's mastery of texture, color, and continuity of bloom. Although few photographs of the garden survive from this period, her

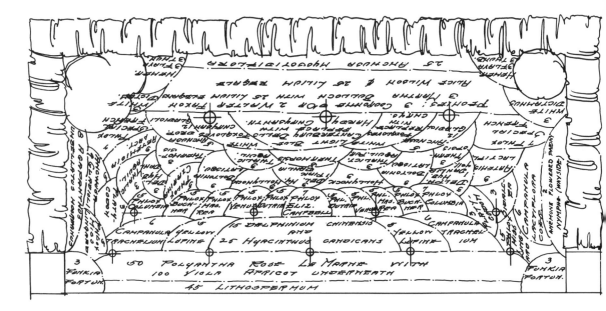

Planting plan for formal garden (detail), prepared by Ellen Shipman, September 1935

written recommendations reveal the full, rich interplay of bloom and foliage characteristic of her best work.

Looking south from the pergola in early July, visitors would have seen, in the foreground, a long border of *Nepeta Mussinii*—catmint—with its gray-green foliage and clouds of tiny mauve blossoms. This frosty border heightened the color values behind. The blooms on the four stands of German iris ('Princess Beatrice,' 'Ambassadeur,' 'Queen Caterina,' and 'Candlelight') faded after a May-June display, but their swordlike, gray-green foliage would remain to punctuate the more spectacular Japanese iris. Three three-foot clumps of the orchid-like flowers, in shades of purple, blue, and white, would have hovered between mounds of white baby's breath. (Shipman's plans always indicated dense planting; six plants of *Gypsophilia* were required to fill a space of about two by two feet.) Behind the iris, tall stands of yellow hollyhock, light blue *Campanula lactiflora* 'Caerulea,' electric blue *Anchusa*, *Phlox* 'Merrell,' and soft yellow *Thermopsis* would also have been in bloom. Most of the plants in the new design were perennials, supplemented with tender bulbs, including gladioli, dahlia, and agapanthus. Blue violas were recommended as underplanting in the four rose beds at the garden's south end, near the teahouse.

The sheer volume of plants was astounding. In just the one bed at the southwest corner of the pool—an area covering about 450 square feet—Shipman's list called for over six hundred plants. These included *Hosta*, *Lithosperum*, polyantha rose, *Anchusa*, white *Dictamus*, *Campanula*, *Delphinium chinensis*, yellow lupine, six varieties of phlox, *Thalictrum*, *Boltonia*, *Artemisia*, hollyhock, white

Elizabeth Mather in formal garden, after 1935

Formal garden path, after 1935

Pergola in formal garden, 1957. Photograph by Walter P. Bruning

Digitalis, Delphinium, daylily, *Lilium elegans, Lilium regale, Platycodon*, and light blue Canterbury bells, which were to be replaced with chrysanthemum each autumn.

Elizabeth and William liked the plan but thought it involved "more expenses for material as well as in labor" than they had anticipated. They asked for a modification, either a "simplification, or perhaps the leaving of some of the panels entirely unplanted,... for example, in grass, as the surroundings of the pool are at present in grass."[2] This solution seems to have been accepted, at least until 1937. Ironically, the panels that remained unplanted were the same ones for which Shipman had designed unexecuted plans twenty-three years before. To cut costs further, Shipman reduced the number of standards in the herbaceous beds; the revised plan used *Wisteria sinensis* and *Viburnum Carlesi* only along the center walkway.

The Mathers considered the proposed design an important addition to Gwinn and reflected carefully on every aspect of it. "As near as we can visualize," William wrote for both of them, "it would represent... a picture of pretty constant bloom of a miscellaneous character, with the bright flower of hollyhock appearing as the raised center of the two panels immediately in front of the pergola, and all... panels raised... from a comparatively low border to a higher center. We think this, if we are right, should produce a pleasant appearance."[3]

They did not, however, approve of the design for the two beds immediately in front of the building, which were to have been filled with primula and chrysanthemum. The low-growing plants would have been invisible from within the pergola, because large marble planters in front obstructed the view of the immediate foreground. So the beds were left as they were until Shipman returned in 1937 to design a new scheme in which they and the walks through them were reconfigured.

The Mathers were also unsure about the use of lilacs at the corners of the pergola, fearing that it would obscure the "architectural effect," and of the tall-growing cedars at the garden's south end, which would obscure the teahouse. Shipman apparently prevailed on this issue, however; both *Syringa* and *Juniperis virginia* are listed on the Wayside Gardens order. Shipman's recommendation for hardy azaleas and cherries in the panels surrounding the pool also raised concern. "I cannot quite visualize the effect which this would have from the pergola where we usually sit, or from the teahouse where we occasionally sit," wrote William.[4] He was worried about the view, which since Platt's time had been open the length of the garden. They initially decided to keep the panels unplanted but changed their minds and adopted Shipman's suggestions in 1937. Four varieties of Japanese cherry, *amanogawa*, *autumnalis*, *Yedoensis Taizanfuken*, and *Hosokawa*, were put in, along with azaleas and Japanese tree lilacs.

Eventually, the tree lilacs grew so large that they forced removal of the smaller trees and shrubs. The character of the central garden gradually shifted from Platt's open, sunny expanse to a shade-dappled grove—an effect that was, ironically, more in keeping with a twentieth-century image of an Italian Renaissance garden, where similarly unchecked growth of overstory trees and sprawling boxwood made flowers scarce.[5]

On 15 May 1936, Ellen Shipman sent Wayside Gardens in Mentor, Ohio, a list of 4,253 plants needed for the new garden: 13 varieties of German iris; 10 of Japanese iris; 16 of garden phlox; 5 of asters; 5 of spirea; 8 of gladiolus; 8 of dahlia; 9 of lilies; 7 of peonies, 5 of clematis, and 3 of campanula, as well as 605 *Nepeta mussinii*, 390 *Primula* 'Munstead' strain, 53 *Gypsophilia*, 60 *Heuchera*, *Juniperus virginia*, pale pink dogwood, and enough hemlocks for a 66-foot hedge.[6] The list did *not* include most of the 469 roses (ordered separately), any of the material already growing in the garden, or that to be raised from seed. The process initiated by Charles Platt decades before had finally been realized.

Formal garden, 1957. Photograph by Walter P. Bruning

Aerial view of Gwinn, from north, ca. 1950

Earlier in the spring of 1936 Mather had directed Manning that, in addition to overseeing the general rehabilitation of the property, his principal task was "to have the formal flower garden developed nicely in accordance with Mrs. Shipman's plans."[7] A sense that his wife wanted to make Gwinn hers no less than his surely influenced William Mather's priorities as he wrote this letter. The stock market crash within months of the Mathers' marriage had clearly hampered Elizabeth's plans for those aspects of Gwinn she could affect—such as linen, dishes, greenhouse flowers, paintings, even planters, all of which were purchased with new circumspection as income shrank. When the Mathers' finances began to improve in the mid-1930s, however, the formal garden offered Elizabeth an opportunity to focus her interests and talents and to strengthen her connection to her new home.

As part of the general restoration at Gwinn, Manning was also asked to advise Luther Webb, the gardener who had succeeded Lillie Jacques Mook, "in regard to the shrubbery and other matters connected with his job." Manning made several recommendations for improvements to the home grounds. The Mathers had decided not to maintain the big wild garden to previous standards. "I presume," Manning wrote to Mather, "it is your desire to adhere to the original intent of the planting."[8] Mather assured him that it was.

Under Manning's supervision, throughout the grounds, branches were trimmed to open up views to the house portico, to distant outlooks along the bluff-top walk, and to the house. In the original wild garden, trees that were crowding better specimens or ruining sight lines were cut. Several weed trees, including cottonwoods and *Ailanthus* were removed from the shore amphitheater. The pachysandra under the Norway maple allée had encroached on the path, narrowing it to three feet; Manning ordered it brought back to five. Some of the more crowded shrubs on the bluff top were grubbed out; evergreen ferns were planted, and the myrtle and pachysandra that had crept in were removed.

The entry, too, received attention. Honeysuckle and forsythia along the drive were pruned; lilacs and Japanese yews were planted at either side of the house entrance. Manning proposed "two good ten foot plants of the Pyramidal Arbor Vitae to be used in place of the shabby Retinospora at the outside of the entrance gate" and singled out a tall white pine at the terminus of the entrance drive—"a notable avenue end"—to be liberated from crowding by several small trees, including a crab, two sumacs, and a mock orange.[9]

Manning suggested that the original wild garden (which he had come to refer to as "the fountain garden") be renewed with five hundred plants from the woods across the boulevard. The broad-leaved evergreens had once again become leggy and weak. He recommended transplanting *Rhododendron maximum*, *carolina*, other rhododendron hybrids, mountain laurel, and *Leucothoe catesbaei* to the ailing grove. But Mather said he was not prepared to pay the estimated fifteen hundred dollars it would cost and instructed Manning instead to buy small nursery-grown shrubs, which would be less expensive to install. The days of large-scale collecting and planting had ended. To further rejuvenate the area Manning also recommended that all its beds be covered with ivy and *Helleborus niger* and that more variety, including primrose and lily-of-the-valley, be used in the beds to the south. These changes marked the final phase of evolution in Manning's original wild garden planting scheme.

In May 1936 Mather wrote to ask Manning for a photograph: "You have been so helpful to me, both at Ishpeming and at Gwinn, that I wish to have a good picture of yourself which I can frame properly and hang one in my house and one at Cliffs Cottage." Manning sent the photos and wrote in return: "I

Path to gate on Lake Shore Boulevard, 1957. Photograph by Walter P. Bruning

would like very much to have a picture of you for my room as you have been one of my most valued friends for so many years."[10] No other of Manning's clients had been with him from the very first years of his practice to the very last, and no others had worked with him on so many projects. Mather and Manning's had been a rich collaboration, temperamentally unlikely, yet genuinely felt and, as the years wore on, increasingly meaningful to both men. In June 1937 Mather wrote that "he had read with interest" his friend's last letters, in which Manning may have raised again the question of Gwinn's future. "Your opinion on all these matters—dreams though some of them may be, yet we should all have dreams—are always welcome with me."[11]

Manning made his last visit to Gwinn in May of 1937. Within one year he suffered three heart attacks, the last of which was fatal. Manning traced his heart trouble to a "fast cliff climb with two younger men" he had taken in 1935.[12] At his death in February 1938, he was still hard at work on his autobiography. Most of his landscape activity had ceased years before.

Together Warren Manning and William Mather had discovered friendship, collegiality, and artistic inspiration. They had explored the potential of landscape for pursuits relating to business and pleasure. At the time of Manning's death, they had known each other for more than forty years.

Manning would have spent some of his last visit to Gwinn in the big wild garden he had worked so long to create. Few people today can visualize what he might have seen on that last tramp through the woods. One who still remembers is Cornelia Ireland, wife of Elizabeth's son, James.

"Each rill needlepointed in fern or bulb was of the greatest delicacy—like the effect of meticulously plumaged wild birds. What you would gasp at today, I think—is how breathlessly refined all the species were, compared to today's hybrids and developments—and how perilously sheer the little banks were. The meticulous early laying out eventuated in pure Quails' Breast fern, multiplying by—it had to be!—heaven's grace. It was very, truly awe inspiring to walk through in May and June . . . then high weeds cloaked everything over. . . . You may well believe each bank was Mr. Mather's joy—I think, almost more than the formal garden beds, much as he loved fountains and the architectural detail . . . —with its beeches, birches, and clouds of fern and (cursed) aegepodium, it was extraordinary, just as one might expect in painting, rather than nature alone."[13]

And herein lies the magic and the paradox of Gwinn. Warren Manning, the "naturalist," planted beeches, birches, and clouds of fern so convincingly that to many eyes, they seemed more like art than nature. Charles Platt, the "classicist," used his artistic skills to deliver the drama of Lake Erie into the heart of the designed landscape. Unexpectedly, their aesthetic territories had crossed. The dichotomy between art and nature—perhaps illusory after all—had been resolved.

Bamboo glade, wild garden, ca. 1930

EPILOGUE

The postwar period at Gwinn saw few physical changes but much enjoyment of the landscape at its peak of maturity. Many civic, Garden Center, and museum-related events were held there, as were intimate dinners with the Mathers' friends.[1] Photographs from the period record a landscape of charm and substance. The Dutch elm blight had not yet stripped the driveway of its magnificent canopy; the Lombardy poplars from earlier plantings still survived, including those in the vista across Lake Shore Boulevard; the flower garden bloomed abundantly under Elizabeth's care.

In 1940, Ellen Shipman returned again to Gwinn to design a parterre for the grass panels in the formal garden. In it William and Elizabeth Mather's initials would intertwine. The design brought the story full circle: these were the beds Shipman had first designed back in 1914. The elegant calligraphy repeated Platt's original monogram, the same insignia that appeared on Gwinn's iron gates. The "WGM" and "ERM" were set into grass, realized in ivy and *Ageratum*.

Shipman created one last design for Gwinn, in March 1946, for the inner beds in front of the pergola. Her three-part scheme consisted of spring bulbs, summer annuals, and chrysanthemums for fall color. Existing borders of barberry, catmint, *Heuchera rosa*, Japanese anemone, columbine, Madonna lilies, and *Lillium speciosum* in these beds were retained. Eight heliotrope and four wisteria standards and two *Prunus amanogawa* were added to echo the careful geometry of the purple, mauve, white, pale pink, and yellow bloom.

Ellen Shipman's contributions to Gwinn were circumscribed but exquisite. The ample documentation of her planting plans makes their eventual restoration an intriguing possibility.

After a slow decline in health, William Mather died at Gwinn in 1951 at the age of ninety-three. He had lived on the estate for forty–three years. Front–page

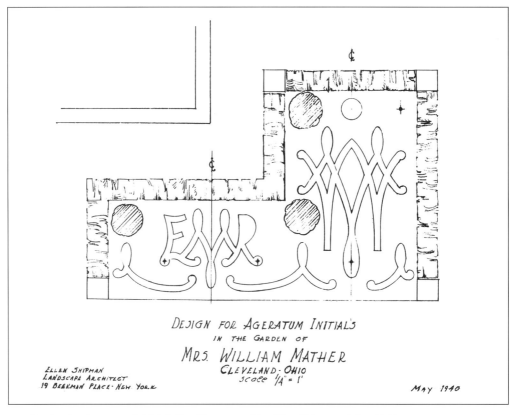

"Design for Ageratum Initials" (detail), prepared by Ellen Shipman, May 1940

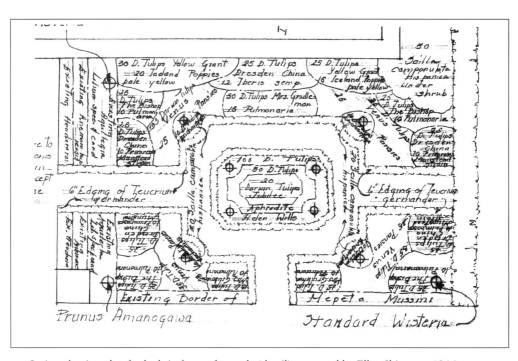

Spring planting plan for beds in front of pergola (detail), prepared by Ellen Shipman, 1946

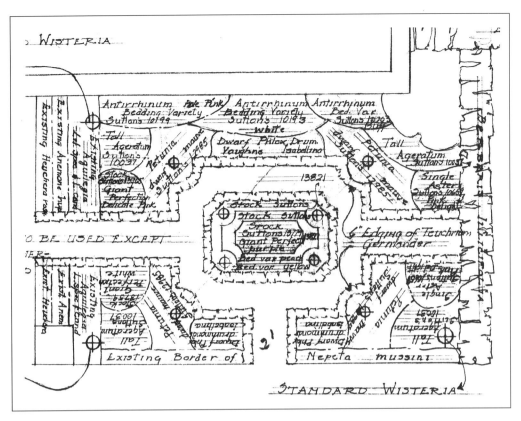

Summer planting plan for beds in front of pergola (detail), prepared by Ellen Shipman, 1946

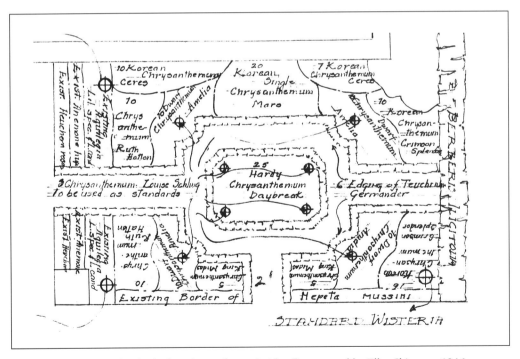

Autumn planting plan for beds in front of pergola (detail), prepared by Ellen Shipman, 1946

articles in the city's newspapers recounted his business accomplishments, honorary degrees, and charitable donations. Mather had made a difference in the community in which he had lived. He died a much-admired, much-loved man.

Elizabeth outlived William by only six years. During that time she continued to entertain exuberantly. Her last celebration was one of the most poetic. In 1957 two hundred and thirty people were invited to Gwinn to dine after an area meeting of the Garden Club of America. "Tables were set on the portico and in a...square around the fountain," one of the evening's guests remembered.[2] "The basin was filled with floating waterlilies. More tables were placed against the balustrades on this level and on the lower platform and on the walks which led to the gazebos. It was an incredibly beautiful evening." Elizabeth was too ill to attend the dinner but made an appearance at the surprise performance that followed.

"The guests went to the south side of the house; the greensward and the long allée of poplars across Lake Shore Boulevard were beautifully illuminated. The formal garden on one side and the wildflower garden on the other glowed with soft light. A great floral garland hung from a lofty elm, suspended from the upper limbs, gently swinging in the evening breeze. There was a rectangle of white on the lawn before which seats had been placed for the guests. Mrs. Mather had brought the premier danseur and the premiere danseuse of the New York [City] Ballet to cap the occasion.... Their movements seemed as elemental as the breeze itself." Elizabeth Mather quietly greeted a few people nearby and

William G. Mather in formal garden, after 1935

The Muses of Gwinn

then returned upstairs. She died three months later, having lived at Gwinn for nearly three decades.

Gwinn is one of the few landscapes from the American Country Place Era to survive relatively intact. The original home grounds retain nearly all of Charles Platt's original architectural elements, largely owing to restorations supervised by Platt, Wyckoff and Coles, the successors of the architect's original practice. Over the years, economic necessity has required some deviation from Warren Manning's planting recommendations. The formal garden has been simplified much as it was by William and Elizabeth Mather during lean times and a new planting scheme for the beds introduced. Several acres of the big wild garden south of boulevard were sold in 1947 when the freeway was constructed. Since that time, the area has not been maintained. Few of the original plantings survive.

Before her death Elizabeth Mather, with her son and her daughter-in-law, James and Cornelia Ireland, arranged to make the estate available to nonprofit organizations as a small conference center, thus keeping alive the family's philanthropic spirit. For the next thirty years, James and Cornelia continued to care for Gwinn, overseeing the grounds, undertaking repairs, and enjoying the estate's new role in the community. In 1988, the second generation of Irelands stepped in to continue the family's management role.

Today, guests wander through Gwinn's house and grounds as they discuss their work. Under the pergola, they discover a rare sense of elegance and calm, unchanged since William and Elizabeth Mather's time. Looking out over the lake, they might see the sun set or a storm race in from the west. Few of Gwinn's visitors know the names of Charles Platt, Warren Manning, and Ellen Shipman, but they do know that they are in a special place, one that invites reflections on beauty, in art and nature.

Yet nature is made better by no mean
But nature makes that mean: so, over that art
Which, you say, adds to nature, is an art
That nature makes.

William Shakespeare, *The Winter's Tale*

APPENDIX I

Warren Manning's projects in the Cleveland area

Compiled from the Client List in the Warren H. Manning Collection, University of Massachusetts at Lowell. (Names are reproduced as they appear on the client list.)

1897: John D. Rockefeller, Forest Hill, Cleveland

1901: L. E. Holden, Cleveland

1902: L. D. Holden, Cleveland

1905: Wade Cemetery, Lakeview Cemetery, Cleveland

1906: J. H. Wade, Gates Mills

1907: M. A. Merrill, Gates Mills

1908: Cleveland Museum of Art, Wade Park, Cleveland
William G. Mather, Cleveland

1912: Samuel C. Mather, Cleveland
Dr. Dudley P. Allen, Cleveland
Severence Estate, Cleveland

1913: Western Reserve University, Cleveland
Samuel Mather (Shoreby), Cleveland
Andrew Squire, Gates Mills
H. G. Dalton, Cleveland

1915: Mayfield Community Lands Subdivision, Cleveland
Samuel Mather, Euclid Ave., Cleveland
Henry S. Sherman, Cleveland
S. Livingston Mather, Little Mountain
Mather, Herrick and Newcomer, Gates Mills

1916: Dr. Bishop, Gates Mills
E. A. Merritt, Gates Mills
A. S. Mather, Gates Mills
Ralph King, F. C. Newcome, Gates Mills
Myron A. Wick, Gates Mills
Dr. G. W. Crile, Cleveland
A. S. Newberry, Cleveland

1917: C. E. Sullivan, Gates Mills
Howard P. Ellis, Cleveland
J. H. Hord, Gates Mills
F. A. Scott, Cleveland
Community Lands, Cleveland
Mrs. D. S. Blossom, Cleveland

1919: E. S. Burke, Chagrin Falls
Chester C. Bolton, Cleveland
Chagrin Hunt Club, Gates Mills
The Pioneer Colonials, Cleveland
Windsor T. White, Chagrin Falls
Alva Bradley, Gates Mills

1920: The Suburban Development Company, Cleveland
C. W. Callacott, Cleveland
Mrs. E. S. Burke, Jr., Cleveland
Dr. William Thomas Corbett, Cleveland
Whitney Warner, Cleveland
Mr. J. A. Miller, Cleveland

1921: A. E. R. Sneider, Cleveland

1922: William M. Clapp, Cleveland Heights

1923: Leonard C. Hanna, Jr., Mentor

1927: Mrs. Flora Kauffholtz, Cleveland
C. E. Sullivan, Subdivision, Cleveland

1928: George A. Martin, Cleveland

1929: F. C. Newcomer, South Woodland
Rd. Extension, Chagrin Valley
F. C. Newcomer, Hillbrook Estates,
Hunting Valley
Miss Selma V. Sullivan, Cleveland

1930: C. E. Sullivan, River Development,
Cleveland
C. E. Sullivan, Snake Hill, Cleveland

1931: Frank C. Newcomer, Hostetler Land,
Gates Mills

1936: Mrs. William G. Mather Estate,
Cleveland [Author's note: This
entry is probably associated with
the unpublished Gwinn narrative.]

APPENDIX II

Ellen Shipman's plant list for the formal garden, based on her Wayside Gardens Order, 15 May 1936

Plant names are given here as they appear on Shipman's plant orders, except that obvious misspellings have been corrected. (Shipman's use of uppercase and lowercase spellings has also been preserved.)

Order #4298

12 Cedar Juniperus virginiana
4 Dogwood (pale pink)
2 Malus floribunda (bush form)
2 Prunus Amanogawa
6 Prunus Autumnalis
3 Prunus Yedoensis Taizanfuken
2 Prunus Hosokawa
6 Buddleia Davidii
4 Bechtel's Crab
6 Syringa Josikaea
3 Viburnum Carlesii (standard form)
20 Hemlocks
6 Taxus cuspidata 'Capitata'
1 Wisteria sinensis (standard form)
1 Hybrid Clematis Ramona
2 Hybrid Clematis montana rubens
2 Hybrid Clematis Jackmanii
2 Hybrid Clematis Mme B. Villard
1 Hybrid Clematis Duchess of Edinburgh
12 Roses Duchess of Wellington
12 Roses E.G. Hill
12 Roses Lady Hillingdon
12 Roses Lady Margaret Stewart
12 Roses Ville de Paris
3 Prunus Yedoensis Taizanfuken
7 Althea

Order #1824

50 AQUILEGIA CHRYSANTHA
50 ANEMONE ALBA
15 ARTEMISIA LACTIFLORA
28 ASTER TATARICUS
10 BOCCONIA CORDATA
20 BOLTONIA LATISQUAMA
12 DICENTRA SPECTABILIS
6 CAMPANULA LACTIFLORA
  'CAERULEA'
30 CAMPANULA PERSICIFOLIA BLUE
10 CIMICIFUGA RACEMOSA
12 DELPHINIUMS WAYSIDE GARDEN
  HYB
16 FUNKIA LANCIFOLIA
10 FUNKIA SUBCORDATA
  GRANDIFLORA
12 HEMEROCALLIS FLAVA
12 HEMEROCALLIS THUNBERGII
14 HOLLYHOCKS MIXED
18 DELPHINIUMS BELLADONNA
3 IRIS GERMAN BALLERINE
3 IRIS GERMAN LENT A
  WILLIAMSON
3 IRIS GERMAN MOTHER OF PEARL
3 IRIS GERMAN PRINCESS BEATRICE
3 IRIS GERMAN PRIMROSE
11 IRIS JAP FASCINATION
10 IRIS JAP GOLDBOUND
11 IRIS JAP LA TOSCA

11 IRIS JAP QUEEN OF THE BLUES
11 LUPINUS YELLOW
40 LUPINUS WAYSIDE GARDEN HYB
500 NEPETA MUSSINII
140 PRIMULA MUNSTEAD STRAIN
5 PHLOX CLARINIA
30 PHLOX L'ESPERANCE (AMERICAN)
40 PHLOX STALLARIA
28 PHLOX DAWN
36 PHLOX DUTRIE
12 PHLOX COLUMBIA
10 PHLOX MRS REA
12 SPIREA GLADSTONE
18 SIDALCEA ROSY GEM
12 THERMOPSIS CAROLINIANA
52 VIOLAS ROSINA
52 VIOLAS ODORATA DOUBLE
   RUSSIAN
15 ACONITUM AUTUMNALE
100 AQUILEGIA SCOTT ELLIOTT HYB
30 AQUILEGIA CHRYSANTHA
84 ANCHUSA DROPMORE
75 ANCHUSA MYOSOTIDIFLORA
60 ANEMONE HUPEHENSIS
30 ANEMONE JAPANESE
3 ARTEMISIA LACTIFLORA
8 ASTERS BARR PINK
8 ASTERS BLUE GEM
11 ASTERS BLIMAX
3 ASTERS LADY LLOYD
3 ASTERS QUEEN MARY
6 SPIREA BETSY CUPERUS
16 SPIREA GRUNO
16 SPIREA FILIPENDULA
9 SPIREA KRIEMHILDE
10 SPIREA PALMATA ELEGANS
10 BOCCONIA CORDATA
17 BOLTONIA LATISQUAMA
10 CAMPANULA LACTIFLORA
   'CAERULEA'
20 CAMPANULA PERSICIFOLIA ALBA
13 CAMPANULA PERSICIFOLIA
   CAERULEA
15 MUMS ULIGINOSUM
12 MUMS HARDY YELLOW
   NORMANDIE

12 MUMS HARDY WHITE
   NORMANDIE
12 CIMICIFUGA RACEMOSA
38 DELPHINIUMS BELLADONNA
42 DELPHINIUMS WAYSIDE GARDEN
   HYB
35 DELPHINIUMS CHINESE
6 DICTAMUS ALBA
3 EUPHORBIA COROLLATA
10 FUNKIA LANCIFOLIA
13 FUNKIA FORTUNEI
53 GYPSOPHILIA BRISTOL FAIRY
15 HEMEROCALLIS FLAVA
15 HEMEROCALLIS THUNBERGII
60 HEUCHERA ROSAMUNDI
17 HOLLYHOCKS YELLOW DOUBLE
16 HOLLYHOCKS PINK DOUBLE
17 HOLLYHOCKS ROSE DOUBLE
10 IRIS GERMAN AMBASSADEUR
6 IRIS GERMAN CANDLELIGHT
10 IRIS GERMAN LORD OF JUNE
16 IRIS GERMAN PRINCESS BEATRICE
10 IRIS GERMAN QUEEN CATERINA
10 IRIS GERMAN SHEKINAH
10 IRIS GERMAN SNOW WHITE
12 IRIS JAP ALBATROSS
12 IRIS JAP COLUMBIA
12 IRIS JAP FASCINATION
12 IRIS JAP GOLDBOUND
12 IRIS JAP MATCHLESS
12 IRIS JAP QUEEN OF THE BLUES
20 LUPINIS WAYSIDE GARDEN HYB
104 NEPETA MUSSINII
18 PAPAVER FAIRY
6 PAPAVER MAY SADLER
19 PAPAVER MRS PERRY
8 PAPAVER PERRYS WHITE
3 PEONIES ALBERT CROUSSE
3 PEONIES ALSACE LORRAINE
6 PEONIES FESTIVA MAXIMA
6 PEONIES MARTHA BULLOCH
6 PEONIES SOLANGE
2 PEONIES SOUVENIR DE LOUIS
   BIGOT
5 PEONIES WALTER FAXON
8 PHLOX ANTONIN MERCIER

24 PHLOX COLUMBIA
10 PHLOX CZARINA
25 PHLOX DAWN
8 PHLOX MME PAUL DUTRIE
7 PHLOX FRAU BUCHNER
3 PHLOX C B MERRELL
25 PHLOX MISS LINGARD
10 PHLOX MRS REA
250 PRIMULA MUNSTEAD STRAIN
15 SIDALCEA ROSY GEM
36 STATICE LATIFOLIA
20 THALICTRUM AQUILEGIFOLIUM
12 THALICTRUM AQUILEGIFOLIUM
    PURPUREUM
6 THALICTRUM GLAUCUM
47 THERMOPSIS CAROLINIANA
9 TROLLIUS LEMON QUEEN
6 VALERIANA COCCINEA
13 PHLOX CREPUSCULE
19 PHLOX DOLLY
24 PHLOX EUGENE
    DANZANVILLIERS
5 PHLOX L'EVENEMENT
10 PHLOX MICHAEL BUCHNER
3 PHLOX PROGRESS
2 DAHLIA MARATHON YELLOW
3 JERSEY'S SWEETHEART PINK
12 GLAD GOLDEN MEASURE
12 GLAD ALBATROS
12 GLAD GIANT NYMPH
50 LILIUM REGALE
24 LILIUM AURATUM MAMMOTH
2 DAHLIA ST FRANCIS WHITE
2 DAHLIA JERSEY'S BEAUTY PINK

2 DAHLIA JERSEY'S IDEAL PINK
2 DAHLIA MARGARET W WILSON
    PINK
2 DAHLIA AVALON YELLOW
2 DAHLIA LEMONADE YELLOW
25 GLAD GOLDEN MEASURE
    YELLOW
25 GLAD PANAMA PINK
25 GLAD PINK WONDER DEEP PINK
25 GLAD SCHWABEN PALE YELLOW
25 GLAD PRIMROSE PRINCESS PALE
    YELLOW
25 GLAD CORYPHEE PINK & WHITE
25 GLAD GIANT NYMPH PINK
25 GLAD GOLDEN DREAM DEEP
    YELLOW
25 GLAD W H PHIPPS PINK
25 GLAD ALBATROS WHITE
25 GLAD MRS H E BOTHLIN PALE
    PINK
72 LILIUM CANDIDUM RUSSIAN
    MAMMOTH
24 LILIUM LONGIFLORUM
    GIGANTEUM
50 LILIUM REGALE
24 LILIUM AURATUM MAMMOTH
55 LILIUM SPECIOSUM ALBUM
    MAMMOTH
80 LILIUM SPECIOSUM RUBRUM
    MAMMOTH
52 VIOLAS ROSINA
3 EUPHORBIA COROLLATA
24 LILIES LONGIFLORUM
    GIGANTEUM

APPENDIX III

The plants of the big wild garden and their locations, based on Warren Manning's list, ca. 1930

Plant names (both Latin and common) are reproduced as they appear on Manning's list, except that obvious misspellings have been corrected.

Abies Fraseri (Fraser fir), the woods, Elm Gate Steps, Bluff Top Path
Acer Negundo (boxelder), Birch Path
Acer rubrum (red maple), the woods
Acer saccharum (sugar maple), the woods
Achillea Millefolium (common yarrow), the fields
Achillea Ptarmica (pearl sneezewort), Field Edge Path
Adiantum pedatum (American maidenhair fern), the woods
Aegopodium Podagraria (goutweed), the woods
Aegopodium Podagraria variegata (variegated goutweed), Field Edge Path
Agrimonia Eupatoria (agrimony), the woods
Agrostis palustris (redtop), Coit Field
Allium canadense (meadow garlic), the woods on Leeks Path
Allium cernuum (nodding onion), Ridge Path
Allium Moly (lily leek), Leeks Path
Althea officinalis (marsh mallow), Mallow Path
Alyssum saxatile (goldentuft), Rockery
Ampelopsis quinquefolia (Virginia creeper), the woods
Amphicarpaea monoica (hog peanut), the woods at Elm Gate Steps
Anaphalis margaritacea (pearl everlasting), the fields
Apocynum cannabinum (hemp dogbane), Coit Field
Aquilegia canadensis (American columbine), the woods
Arabis albida (rock cress), the rock garden
Aralia chinensis mandahurica (Mandahurica aralia), the woods on Wild Plum Path
Aralia nudicaulis (wild sarsaparilla), the woods
Aralis racemosa (American spikenard), the woods
Arisaema triphyllum (Jack-in-the-pulpit), the woods
Aruncus sylvester (common goatsbeard), the woods
Arundinaria falcata (Ningala bamboo), Bamboo Path
Arundinaria macrosperma (southern cane), Bamboo Path
Asarum canadense (Canada wild ginger), Ginger Root Path

Asclepias syriaca (common milkweed), Coit Field
Asclepias tuberosa (butterfly weed), Field Edge Path
Asimina triloba (pawpaw), the woods on Pawpaw Path
Asplenium platyneuron (ebony spleenwort), the woods on Fern Path
Aster cordifolius (blue wood aster), the woods
Aster corymbosus (white wood aster), the woods
Aster grandiflorus (great aster), the woods
Aster laevis (smooth aster), the woods
Aster multiflorus (wreath aster), Coit Field
Aster novae-angliae (New England aster), the woods along Field Edge Path
Aster novae-angliae 'Roseus' (Rosy New England aster), Mallow Path
Aster patens (sky drop aster), Coit Field
Astilbe japonica (Japanese astilbe), the woods on Bamboo Path
Athyrium Filix-femina (lady fern), the woods
Azalea arborescens (sweet azalea), Waterleaf Path
Azalea calendulacea (flame azalea), the woods

Baccaris halimifolia (groundselbush), Salt Marsh Path
Bambusa Metake (arrow bamboo), the woods on Bamboo Path
Bambusa palmata (handleaf bamboo), Bamboo Path
Bambusa pygmaea (carpet bamboo), Bamboo Path
Baptisia australis (blue wild indigo), Field Edge Path
Benzoin aestivale (spicebush), the woods
Betula alba (European white birch), the woods on Birch Path
Boehmeria cylindrica (false nettle), the woods
Botrychium dissectum (cutleaf grape fern), the woods

Carex plantaginea (plantainleaf sedge), moss garden
Carpinus caroliniana (American hornbeam), the woods
Centaurea Cyanus (cornflower), Field Edge Path
Cephalanthus occidentalis (common buttonbush), the woods
Cercis canadensis (American redbud), the woods
Chamaecyparis obtusa 'Nana' (dwarf Hinoki cypress), Birch Path
Chamaecyparis pisifera 'Plumosa' (plume retinospora), the woods on Birch Path
Chamaecyparis pisifera 'Plumosa Aurea' (goldenplume retinospora), the woods on Birch Path
Chamaecyparis pisifera 'Squarrosa' (moss retinospora), the woods on Birch Path
Chrysanthemum Balsamita (costmary), Field Edge Path
Cichorium Intybus (chicory), Field Edge Path
Cimicifuga americana (American bugbane), the woods
Cimicifuga racemosa (Cohosh bugbane), the woods
Cnicus altissima (tall thistle), the woods
Commelina virginica (day-flower), the woods
Cornus paniculata (gray dogwood), the fields
Cryptotaenia canadensis (honewort), the woods
Cypripedium acaule (pink ladyslipper), the woods on Ladyslipper Steps
Cypripedium pubescens (common yellow ladyslipper), the woods on Ladyslipper Steps
Cyrilla racemiflora (cyrilla), the woods

Daucus Carota (Queen Anne's Lace), Coit Field
Dennstaedtia punctilobula (hay-scented fern), the woods on Fern Path
Desmodium canadense (hoary tickclover), the woods on Birch Path
Dianthus barbatus (sweet William), Field Edge Path
Dicentra eximia (fringed bleeding-heart), Bluff Top Path near Iris Path
Dodecatheon Meadia (common shooting-star), Wild Plum Path, Bluff Top Path
Dryopteris Goldiana (goldie fern), the woods
Dryopteris hexagonoptera (winged woodfern), the woods on Fern Path
Dryopteris marginalis (leather woodfern), the woods
Dryopteris noveboracensis (New York fern), the woods on Fern Path
Dryopteris spinulosa (toothed woodfern), the woods

Epilobium angustifolium (blooming Sally), the woods
Equisetum sylvaticum (woodland horsetail), the woods on Cushion Bank Path
Euonymus obovata (running euonymus), Wahoo Path
Eupatorium coelestinuum (mistflower), Twin Elm Steps
Eupatorium perfoliatum (boneset), Joe Pye Walk
Eupatorium purpureum (Joe-Pye weed), Joe Pye Walk, Elm Gate Steps
Eupatorium urticifolium (snow thoroughwort), the woods
Euphorbia Cyparissias (cypress spurge), Field Edge Path
Fagus americana (American beech), the woods, Beech Glade
Fraxinus americana (white ash), the farm woods

Galanthus nivalis (common snowdrop), Wild Plum Path
Galax aphylla (galax), the woods
Galium boreale (bedstraw), Field Edge Path
Gentiana Andrewsii (closed gentian), the woods
Geranium maculatum (wild geranium), the woods, Moss Garden
Geranium Robertianum (herb Robert), the woods, Moss Garden
Geum album (white avena), the woods, Gwinn Vista

Halesia tetraptera (great silverbell), the woods
Helenium autumnale (common sneezeweed), Sunflower Path
Helianthus giganteus (giant sunflower), Sunflower Path
Helianthus mollis (ashy sunflower), Field Edge Path
Helianthus strumosus (woodland sunflower), the woods
Helianthus tuberosus (Jerusalem artichoke), Sunflower Path
Heliopsis helianthoides (sunflower heliopsis)
Hemerocallis Dumortieri (early daylily), Field Edge Path
Hemerocallis flava (lemon daylily), Field Edge Path
Hemerocallis fulva (tawny daylily), the woods on Ribbonleaf Path
Heracleum lanatum (cow parsnip), the woods
Hicoria glabra (pignut), the woods on Birch Path
Hosta caerulea (blue plantainlily), Moss Garden
Hosta lancifolia (lanceleaf plantainlily), Bluff Top Path Bridge
Hosta plantaginea (white plantainlily), Moss Garden
Hosta Sieboldiana (cushion plantainlily), the woods, Moss Garden
Houstonia caerulea (bluets), the woods
Hydrangea arborescens (smooth hydrangea), Bluff Top Path near Elm Gate Steps

Hydrophyllum appendiculatum (broadleaf waterleaf), the woods on Waterleaf Path
Hydrophyllum virginianum (Virginia waterleaf), the woods

Impatiens biflora (spotted snapweed), Jewel Path
Iris Chamaeiris (Crimean iris), Moss Garden
Iris cristata (crested iris), Moss Garden Path
Iris germanica (German iris), Field Edge Path
Iris Kaempferi (Japanese iris), the woods at Elm Gate Path
Iris sibirica (Siberian iris), the woods on Bluff Top and Field Edge Paths

Juglans cinerea (butternut), the woods on Birch Path
Juniperus chinensis (Chinese juniper), the woods, Birch Path

Kniphofia Uvaria (common torchlily), Field Edge Path

Larix europaea (European larch), Birch Path
Lepachys pinnata (lepachys), Field Edge Path
Leucothoe Catesbaei (drooping leucothoe), Waterleaf Path
Leucothoe racemosa (sweetbells), the woods
Ligularia clivorum (orange groundsel), the woods, Ladyslipper Steps
Lillium tigrinum (tiger lily), Field Edge Path
Liriodendron Tulipifera (tuliptree), the woods, the farm woods
Lobelia Cardinalis (cardinal flower), the woods, Moss Garden
Lonicera japonica (Japanese honeysuckle), Field Edge Path
Lygodium palmatum (Hartford fern), the woods
Lysimachia clethroides (clethra loosestrife), the woods, Moss Garden
Lysimachia Nummularia (moneywort), the woods
Lysimachia vulgaris (golden loosestrife), Field Edge Path

Maclura pomifera (Osage orange), Coit Field
Magnolia acuminata (cucumber tree), Field Edge Path
Mahonia Aquifolium (Oregon hollygrape), the woods on Birch Path
Malus Halliana 'Parkmanii' (Parkman crab), Field Edge Path
Mertensia virginica (Virginia bluebells), the woods on Bluebell Path
Mikania scandens (climbing hempweed), along the stream
Monarda didyma (beebalm), the woods on Sunflower Path
Muscari botryoides (common grape hyacinth), Primrose Path at Leatherleaf Path
Muscari botryoides alba (white grape hyacinth), Primrose Path at Leatherleaf Path
Myosotis scorpioides semperflorens (dwarf perpetual forget-me-nots), the woods

Narcissus Jonquilla (jonquil), the woods on Primrose Path
Narcissus poeticus (poets narcissus), Primrose Path at Bluff Top Path
Nyssa sylvatica (tupelo), the farm woods

Oenothera biennsis (common evening primrose), the woods
Ophioglossum vulgatum (common adderstongue), the woods
Opuntia missouriensis (Missouri prickly pear), Rock Garden
Ornithogalum umbellatum (common star-of-Bethlehem), Wild Plum Path
Osmunda cinnamomea (cinnamon fern), the woods on Primrose and Fern Paths
Osmunda regalis (royal fern), the woods in glade west of Ladyslipper Steps
Ostrya virginiana (American hophornbeam), the woods near vista and seat

Panax quinquefolius (American ginseng), Jewel Path, Bluff Top Path
Periploca graeca (Grecian silk vine), Field Edge Path
Phlox divaricata (blue phlox), the woods
Phlox paniculata (garden phlox), Field Edge Path
Physostegia virginiana (Virginia false dragonhead), Field Edge Path
Pilea pumila (richweed), the woods
Pinus montana (Swiss mountain pine), the woods on Birch Path
Pinus Mugo (Hill's dwarf mugho pine), the woods on Cushion Bank Path
Polygonatum commutatum (great Solomon's-seal), the woods
Polygonum sachalinense (sacaline), Field Edge Path
Polystichum acrostichoides (Christmas fern), Hemlock Path
Populus angulata (Carolina cottonwood), the woods, the farm woods, Sunflower Path
Populus Eugenei (Carolina poplar), Cottonwood Vista
Populus monilifera (northern cottonwood), the woods on Cottonwood Vista
Populus nigra 'Italica' (Lombardy poplar), Gwinn Vista, the fields
Primula acaulis (English primrose), the woods on Primrose Path
Primula japonica (Japanese primrose), Primrose Path
Prunella vulgaris (self-heal), Bluff Top Path
Prunus angustifolia (chicksaw plum), Wild Plum Path
Prunus pensylvanica (pin cherry), the woods
Pteretis nodulosa (ostrich fern), the woods
Pyracantha coccinea (scarlet firethorn), Bluff Top Path at Cottonwood Vista

Quercus macrocarpa (mossy-cup oak), the woods
Quercus palustris (pin oak), the woods at Bluff Top Path
Quercus stellata (post oak), the woods near Coit Field
Quercus velutina (black oak), the woods

Ranunculus repens (creeping buttercup), Wahoo Path
Rhododendron carolinianum (Carolina rhododendron), the woods
Rhododendron catawbiense (catawba rosebay rhododendron), the woods
Rhododendron maximum (rosebay rhododendron), the woods
Rhus Toxicodendron (poison ivy), the woods
Rhus typhina (staghorn sumac), the woods
Robinia Kelseyi (Kelsey locust), the woods on Birch Path
Robinia Pseudoacacia (common locust), Coit Field
Rosa lucida (Virgina rose), Gwinn Vista
Rubus argutus (highbush blackberry), the woods
Rubus procumbens (northern dewberry), Coit Field
Rudbeckia laciniata (cutleaf coneflower), the woods on Sunflower Path
Rudbeckia speciosa (showy coneflower), Field Edge Path

Sagina subulata (pearlwort), the woods
Sagittaria latifolia (common arrowhead), Moss Garden
Salix alba (white willow), stream edges
Salix fragilis (brittle willow), stream edges
Salix sericea (silky willow), stream edges
Sambucus canadensis (American elder), Elder Path
Sambucus pubens (scarlet elder), Red Elder Path

Sarracenia flava (trumpet pitcherplant), the woods
Sassafras officinale (sassafras), the fields
Scilla hispanica (Spanish squills), Wild Plum Path at Bluff Top
Scilla sibirica (Siberian squills), Primrose Path near Bluff Top
Sedum ternatum (mountain stonecrop), the woods on Fern Path
Silphium perfoliatum (cup roseweed), Field Edge Path
Sium cicutifolium (water parsnip), the woods, Moss Garden Pools
Smilacina racemosa (false Solomon's-seal), the woods
Smilax rotundifolia (common cat briar), the woods on Three Arch Path
Solanum Dulcamara (bitter nightshade), the woods
Solidago caesia (wreath goldenrod), Giant Maple Steps
Solidago canadensis (Canada goldenrod), the woods and fields
Solidago graminifolia (lanceleaf goldenrod), Cushion Bank Path
Solidago latifolia (broadleaf goldenrod), the woods
Solidago nemoralis (Oldfield goldenrod), Coit Field
Staphylea trifolia (American bladdernut), the woods

Tanacetum vulgare crispum (double tansy), Field Edge Path
Thalictrum dioicum (early meadowrue), the woods
Thuja occidentalis (American arborvitae), the woods on Birch Path
Thuja orientalis (Oriental arborvitae), the woods on Birch Path
Tiarella cordifolia (Allegheny foamflower), the woods, Moss Garden
Tilia americana (American linden), the woods, the farm woods
Tradescantia virginiana (Virginia spiderwort), the woods

Ulmus fulva (slippery elm), the woods, Three Arch Bridge
Uvularia sessilifolia (little merrybells), the woods

Vernonia noveboracensis (common ironweed), Field Edge Path
Veronica repens (creeping speedwell), Field Edge Path
Veronica spicata (spike speedwell), Field Edge Path
Veronica spuria (bastard speedwell), Field Edge Path
Viburnum acerifolium (mapleleaf viburnum), the woods
Viola cucullata (blue marsh violet), the woods
Vitis aestivalis (summer grape), the woods

Woodsia ilvensis (rusty woodsia), the woods

Yucca filamentosa (common yucca), Field Edge Path

ACKNOWLEDGMENTS

Of the many people who assisted me in the course of creating this book, none was more helpful than Lucy Ireland Weller, Gwinn's executive director. My profound thanks go to her and the rest of the Ireland family for their support, encouragement, and patience. During many trips to Gwinn, I was shown every kindness by the staff there. Lloyd "Mac" McKenna, Linnea Meaney, and Gwinn's superintendent, William Tepley, shared information generously and helped in numerous ways. I am also grateful to Ruth Levenson, who first took me to Gwinn, and Joanna Bristol of the Cleveland Botanical Garden, who helped me explore the library there.

Ngaere Macray showed great patience as I developed this book under the auspices of Sagapress. She has been an inspiration and a good friend throughout an unexpectedly long process. The trust of the directors of the Library of American Landscape History—Eleanor Ames, Nesta Spink, and John Franklin Miller (who first suggested Gwinn as a subject)—has meant a great deal to me, professionally and personally. I am particularly grateful to LALH president Nancy Turner for her unflagging kindness toward me and for her interest in my work and the Library, generally. I also thank the Library's consultants, especially Judith Tankard and Richard Abel, who had many good words of advice throughout this project.

Keith Morgan has been an invaluable source of information and support throughout this project. He, Judith Tankard, Richard Abel, John Miller, and Martha Mayo read early versions of the manuscript and offered insightful comments. I also thank David Streatfield, a much-valued colleague, whose support and criticism have been crucial, and William Baltz, whose fine photographic reproductions illustrate this volume.

Working with my editor, Carol Betsch, was an unexpected delight. I thank her for her countless helpful suggestions, her flexibility, and her grand abilities as an editor and photographer.

My husband, Michael Karson, also periodically reviewed the text and contributed many excellent, often amusing perspectives on it. My deepest thanks go to him for his encouragement of my passions, whatever they are. I also thank our sons, Ethan Liberty Karson and Max Robinson Karson, for their unfailing irreverence and good humor.

Research for this monograph was supported by generous grants from the Elizabeth Ring Mather and William Gwinn Mather Fund and the National Endowment for the Arts, a federal agency. The Garden Conservancy facilitated sponsorship of my early research.

NOTES

All correspondence not otherwise cited is in the William Gwinn Mather Papers, Gwinn Archives, Gwinn Estate, Cleveland, Ohio (abbreviated WGM).

The major archive for Ellen Shipman is the Ellen McGowan Biddle Shipman Papers, Department of Manuscripts and University Archives, Cornell University Libraries, Ithaca, New York (abbreviated SPC).

Warren Manning's papers and autobiography (cited as WMA followed by chapter number—when available—and page number) are in the Warren Manning Collection, Center for Lowell History, University of Massachusetts at Lowell, Lowell, Massachusetts (abbreviated MCL).

CHAPTER ONE

1. Gwinn's archives document Ellen Shipman's work on the formal garden in 1914, 1935, 1936, 1940, and 1946.
2. Melville Chater, "Ohio, The Gateway State," *National Geographic*, May 1932, 530.
3. "The House of William G. Mather," *Architectural Record* 26 (November 1909): 13.
4. *National Architect,* September 1912, 22; Frank Miles Day, ed., *American Country Houses of To-day* (New York: Architectural Book Publishing, 1912); Aymar Embury II, "Charles A. Platt: His Work," *Architecture* 26 (August 1912): 130–62; *Country Life in America*, September 1912, 28–30.
5. Royal Cortissoz, *Monograph of the Work of Charles A. Platt with an Introduction by Royal Cortissoz* (New York: Architectural Book Publishing, 1913), v.
6. Louise Shelton, *Beautiful Gardens in America* (New York: Charles Scribner's Sons, 1915); Samuel Howe, ed., *American Country Houses of To-day* (New York: Architectural Book Publishing, 1915).
7. Albert Davis Taylor, *The Complete Garden* (Garden City, N.Y.: Doubleday, 1921); Eunice Fenelon, "Open House in the Gardens of Greater Cleveland," *Your Garden and Home*, June 1934, 13; James M. Fitch and F. F. Rockwell, *Treasury of American Gardens* (New York: Harper and Brothers, 1956).
8. Samuel Howe, "Gwinn, Cleveland, U.S.A.," *Country Life*, May 1916, 565.
9. *Town and Country*, April 1915.

CHAPTER TWO

1. The opposing points of view are most concisely presented by William Robinson in *The Wild Garden* (1870) and by Reginald Blomfield and F. Inigo Thomas in *The Formal Garden in England* (1892). Both books were reprinted by Sagapress and are distributed by Timber Press.
2. Mrs. Schuyler Van Rensselaer, *Art Out-of-Doors: Hints on Good Taste in Gardening*, 2d ed.

(New York: Charles Scribner's Sons, 1903), 160, 185, 157, 60. There were certainly other writers who addressed the issue of formal versus informal style before Van Rensselaer, including, primarily, Andrew Jackson Downing. I began the discussion here, in 1893, because the aesthetic considerations of country house design began to change radically in the early 1890s.

3. Horace J. McFarland, "An American Garden," *Outlook*, October 1899, 327–33. The estate belonged to Clement Griscom and was located outside Philadelphia. The project began under the auspices of the Olmsted firm.

4. George Pentecost, "The Formal and the Natural Style," *Architectural Record* 12 (June 1902): 174–94.

5. Wilhelm Miller, *What England Can Teach Us about Landscape Gardening* (New York: Doubleday, Page, 1911), v; idem, *The Prairie Spirit in Landscape Gardening*, circular no. 184, Agricultural Experiment Station, Department of Horticulture, University of Illinois, Urbana, 1915, quoted in Christopher Vernon, "William Miller: Prairie Spirit in Landscape Gardening," in *Shaping Heartland Landscapes*, ed. William Tishler, (New York: Sagapress in association with Library of American Landscape History, forthcoming). I am grateful to Christopher Vernon for making his chapter available to me in manuscript.

6. Robert E. Grese, *Jens Jensen: Maker of Natural Parks and Gardens* (Baltimore: Johns Hopkins University Press, 1992), 28. Grese's book offers an excellent overview of Jensen's career.

7. In this respect, Manning resembled his mentor, F. L. Olmsted. See Frederick Law Olmsted, "Foreign Plants and American Scenery," *Garden and Forest* 1 (October 1888): 418.

8. Guy Lowell, *American Gardens* (Boston: Bates and Guild, 1902).

9. Charles A. Platt, "Where We Get Our Ideas of Country Places in America," *The Outing*, June 1904, 351.

10. Herbert Croly, "The Architectural Work of Charles A. Platt," *Architectural Record* 15 (March 1904): 181–244. Interestingly, Croly argued that by modeling his landscape approach on that of Italian Renaissance architects, Platt had resolved the stylistic dilemma between formal and informal design. Croly maintained that the tension between the two had arisen "only during a recent period, when the 'formal' garden, as transplanted to England, became rigid and stiff." The gardens of Italy, Croly continued, "formal as they were, were designed with an eye strictly to landscape values, and constitute without doubt the supremely happy blending of architectural propriety and out-of-door feeling" (183).

   In one respect, Platt *had* bridged the gap between art and nature simply by choosing to design the house and garden as a unit. But creating an "out-of-door" feeling was not Platt's strength or the focus of his major interest. Thus Platt was accurately perceived by critics and clients to occupy the formal end of the landscape spectrum, just as Manning was considered to represent a naturalistic approach even though he accommodated his clients' wishes for geometric formality.

11. Harold D. Eberlein, "Some Recent Aspects of Garden Design," *Architectural Record* 37 (April 1915): 308. Eberlein applauded the movement away from the strictly formal garden: "The majority of garden owners are happily getting beyond the stage where they desire gardens planned to impress the approaching stranger by their starched, smug, symmetrical ostentation" (304).

12. Mark Alan Hewitt, *The Architect and the American Country House* (New Haven: Yale University Press, 1990). Hewitt's scholarly overview of the country house movement is an invaluable source of information for the specialist, although his treatment of the period's landscapes is not the book's strength.

13. The term was first proposed by Norman Newton, *Design on the Land: The Development of Landscape Architecture* (Cambridge: Harvard University Press/Belknap Press, 1971), and has since been widely accepted.

14. Herbert Croly [A. C. David, pseud.], "New Phases in Domestic Architecture," *Architectural Record* 26 (November 1909): 308.

CHAPTER THREE

1. Keith N. Morgan, *Charles A. Platt, The Artist as Architect* (New York and Cambridge: Architectural History Foundation and MIT Press, 1985). I have drawn heavily on Morgan's excellent biography of Platt for this portrait of the designer.

2. Ibid., 15.

3. Ibid., 16.

4. Ibid., 23.

5. Frances Duncan, "The Gardens of Cornish," *Century Magazine*, May 1906, 3–19.

6. Ellen Biddle Shipman, "Garden Note Book," 2, SPC. This undated incomplete manuscript represents one of the few surviving pieces of writing by Shipman.

7. Platt to Stanford White, 29 August 1890, quoted in Morgan, *Platt*, 29.

8. Shipman, "Garden Note Book," 1. Shipman's experience of Platt's design at High Court was also a pivotal moment in her own development: "It was then that I realized that the garden would always be the most important part of a home for me" (1).

9. Frederick Law Olmsted to William Platt, 1 February 1892, quoted in Laura Wood Roper, *FLO, A Biography of Frederick Law Olmsted* (Baltimore: Johns Hopkins University Press, 1973), 433.

10. A reprint of Platt's *Italian Gardens*, with an overview by Keith N. Morgan and additional plates not included in the original 1894 edition, was published in 1993 (Portland, Ore.: Sagapress/Timberpress). Cortissoz defended Platt's "brief and undogmatic" text: "The thing that interested Platt to elucidate for travellers in Italy was the shrewdness with which the Renaissance architects had planned the country palaces of their clients so as to take advantage of every peculiarity of site and to give the princely dweller on some great hillside not only the things that he wanted 'for show' but the things he needed for comfort" (*Monograph*, v).

11. Wharton's *Italian Villas and Their Gardens* was reprinted, with new introductory notes by Henry Hope Reed and Thomas S. Hayes, in 1988 (New York: Classical America/Arthur Ross Foundation).

12. See Richard G. Kenworthy, "Bringing the World to Brookline: The Gardens of Larz and Isabel Anderson" *Journal of Garden History* 11 (1991), and Alan Emmet, "Faulkner Farm: An Italian Garden in Massachusetts," *Journal of Garden History* 6 (April–June 1986).

13. Ralph Adams Cram, "Faulkner Farm, Brookline, Massachusetts," *House and Garden*, August 1901, 1.

14. Hewitt, *Architect*, 64. Hewitt credits Carrère and Hastings as being the first firm to plan estates as integrated formal compositions.

15. Platt, "Where We Get Our Ideas," 349–51.

16. A full analysis of Platt's collaborations with landscape architects has not yet been undertaken. Ellen Biddle Shipman was Platt's most frequent garden design partner, but Olmsted Brothers also worked with him on several projects. Platt and Manning worked together on only one other occasion. According to Manning's autobiography: "Mr. Harold F. McCormick had me consult with Charles Platt his architect in locating his mansion and planning and planting of the grounds of his shore estate, south of Walden. In this property were attractive woodland areas which were left in their natural condition after entrance roads and trails were established" (WMA, 7: 19). See also Manning job list, MCL, job no. 236.

17. Geoffrey Platt, quoted in Morgan, *Platt*, 200.

18. One of Platt's projects for the Astors, New York's Mercantile Building, designed 1911–12, was demolished to make way for the Empire State Building.

19. Charles Downing Lay, "An Interview with Charles A. Platt," *Landscape Architecture* 2 (January, 1912): 127, 130.

20. WMA, 2:1, 1:4. Manning's long manuscript provides a wealth of information about his early years and many of his projects.

21. This number was derived from the "Employee List," WMA. Since several of the employees were listed by surnames and first initials only, this tally may have omitted still others.

22. WMA, 1:2.

23. Ibid., 1:3.

24. Fletcher Steele to John Steele, 27 January 1912. Fletcher Steele Papers, Rochester Historical Society, Rochester, N.Y. Steele's correspondence with his parents offers a unique glimpse into the workings of Manning's Boston office.

25. WMA, 4:1. A account of Olmsted Sr.'s horticultural insecurities is presented by Susan L. Klaus, "Such Inheritance as I Can Give You," *Journal of the New England Garden History Society* 3 (Fall 1993): 1–7.

26. WMA, 4:1.

27. This job—described as "small home grounds"—appears in Manning's client list as no. 20 and is dated 1890.

28. Lance Neckar, "Developing Landscape Architecture for the Twentieth Century: The Career of Warren H. Manning," *Landscape Journal* 8 (Fall 1989): 78–91. Neckar's article is the most comprehensive overview of Manning's accomplishments published to date.

29. WMA, 4:13.

30. Geoffrey Jellicoe and Susan Jellicoe, *The Landscape of Man* (New York: Van Nostrand Reinhold, 1982), 249.

31. WMA, 4:7.

32. Ibid., 4:8.

33. Ibid.

34. It appears that the Mather job must have come into the Olmsted office in 1896 (just before Manning left) and then a three-year hiatus followed. When Mather contacted the Olmsted firm again in 1899, he would have been informed that Manning had left to start his own office. The Mather job listing appears in Manning's office records that year as no. 269; in the Olmsted records it is listed as no. 2225.

35. "Mr. Mather's Cottage and Grove," *Cliffs News*, 1975, unpaginated.

36. This number is based on the client list held in MCL.

37. Warren Manning, "The Purpose and Practice of Landscape Architecture," from *Transactions of the Indiana Horticultural Society for 1893* (Cambridge: Gray Herbarium of Harvard University, 1918), 6.

38. WMA, 7:16.

39. Apparently Manning could not satisfy all the McCormicks' landscape needs, however; in 1902 Ralph Griswold was commissioned to create a formal flower garden for Walden.

40. The estate is now a house museum and open to the public.

41. According to recently discovered plans, paths were laid out through large tracts of woods at Hill-Stead, effectively transforming these into wild gardens; one feature, identified as "the 100 steps," led to a viewing platform not unlike the one Manning later designed for Gwinn. A 1916 planting plan by Beatrix Farrand for the estate's octagonal flower garden also survives.

42. Mac Griswold and Eleanor Weller, *The Golden Age of American Gardens* (New York: Abrams, 1991), 70.

43. Stan Hywet is perhaps the best preserved of Manning's estates. For information about preservation treatment there, see Susan Child, "Warren Manning, 1860–1938: The Forgotten Genius of the American Landscape," *Journal of the New England Garden History Society* 1 (Fall 1991): 29–38; see also note 59, below.

44. Irene Seiberling, interview with author, 18 February 1991, Akron, Ohio.

45. WMA, 7:10.

46. In addition to publishing plant lists of easily grown, locally collectable species for low- and middle–income homeowners, Manning contributed many articles to *Landscape Architecture* and *Country Life in America*, among other journals and newspapers. He directed three magazines (all of which were titled *Billerica*) and coauthored one book, with William Lambeth, *Thomas Jefferson, As an Architect and a Designer of Landscapes* (Boston: Houghton Mifflin, 1913). See Charles A. Birnbaum and Lisa E. Crowder, *Pioneers of American Landscape Design: An Annotated Bibliography* (Washington, D.C.: U.S. Department of the Interior, 1993), 82–86. A shortened version of Manning's National Plan appeared in "A National Plan Study Brief," *Landscape Architecture* 8 (July 1923): 3–24.

47. "Warren H. Manning, Landscape Designer: A Tribute to a Pioneer in a New Profession" (obituary), *Landscape Architecture* 28 (April 1938): 149.

48. Warren Manning, "Report on the Estate of Mr. F. A. Seiberling, Akron, Ohio," 7 November 1928. Archives, Stan Hywet Hall and Gardens, Akron, Ohio.

49. Ellen Biddle Shipman obituary, *New York Times*, 29 March 1950.

50. Shipman, "Garden Note Book," 2 (quotations in the following paragraphs are from the notebook, 3–4).

51. Shipman would later design a planting plan for Aspet's formal garden.

52. See Leslie Rose Close, *The Photographs of Mattie Edwards Hewitt: Portraits of an Era in Landscape Architecture* (New York: Wave Hill, 1983).

53. I have drawn this picture of Shipman's life and practice from several sources, including Deborah Kay Meador, "The Making of a Landscape Architect: Ellen Biddle Shipman and Her Years at the Cornish Colony," Master's thesis, Cornell University, 1989; Leslie Rose Close, "Ellen Biddle Shipman," in *American Landscape Architecture: Designers and Places*, ed. William H. Tishler (Washington, D.C.: Preservation Press, 1989), 90–93; and Daniel Krall, "Early Women Designers and Their Work in Public Places" (paper presented at "Landscapes and Gardens: Women Who Made a Difference" symposium, Michigan State University, East Lansing, June 1987).

54. Shipman, quoted in Anne Petersen, "Women Take Lead in Landscape Art," *New York Times*, 13 March 1938.

55. Shipman to William and Elizabeth Mather, 15 November 1945, SPC.

56. I am grateful to Judith Tankard for making preliminary drafts of her forthcoming biography of Ellen Shipman available to me. This work will be published by Sagapress in 1996.

57. Oversize box, yew, and cedar shrubs are a hallmark of neglected Ellen Shipman gardens. Because designers today rarely interplant evergreens with perennials, Shipman's intention that these large plants be maintained at a perennial scale is often overlooked by gardeners.

58. "House and Garden's Own Hall of Fame," *House and Garden*, June 1933, 50.

59. One fine exception is the English Garden at Stan Hywet, whose planting plans were designed by Shipman ca. 1929; the area recently underwent preservation treatment according to recommendations by Doell and Doell, Syracuse, New York.

1. Timothy J. Loya, "William Gwinn Mather, the Man," *Inland Seas,* Summer 1990, 121.

2. Ibid., 105.

3. Neckar, "Developing Landscape Architecture." Manning was an early advocate of planning on local, regional, and national levels. His concern for using natural and cultural resources to best advantage continued throughout his life.

4. William G. Mather obituary, *Cleveland Plain Dealer,* 7 April 1951.

5. Among Taylor's notable local works are Winding Creek Farm (1926), Daisy Hill Farms (1925), and Peterloon, in nearby Indian Hills, Ohio. In the mid-1930s Taylor redesigned the former Rockefeller estate, Forest Hill, as a city park of national significance and published a substantial report about it in 1938. With his colleagues Taylor prepared more than forty editions of "Construction Notes," published in *Landscape Architecture* from 1935 to 1940. Taylor's book *The Complete Garden* (Garden City, N.Y.: Doubleday, 1921) was illustrated with photographs of Gwinn, among other landscapes. See Noel Dorsey Vernon, "Albert Davis Taylor," in Tishler, *American Landscape Architecture,* 104–7.

6. One of Horvath's apprentices was Elbert Peets, who returned to Cleveland after graduating from Harvard and ran a successful planning office through the 1920s and 1930s. Bryant Fleming, an architect who apprenticed in Manning's Boston office between 1901 and 1904 also worked in Cleveland for several years, designing a large garden in Cleveland for Charles E. Briggs.

7. See Appendix I for a complete list of Manning's Cleveland-area jobs.

8. Alice K. Howell, "Remarks by Charles A. Platt, New York, N.Y." (meeting of Garden Club of Cleveland, 3 August 1912), WGM. Elizabeth Ring Mather later served as president of the club from 1929 to 1931 and president of the Garden Center of Greater Cleveland from 1930 to 1934 and again from 1944 to 1946.

CHAPTER FIVE

1. Manning to Mather, 20 September 1906.

2. Manning to Mather, 14 November 1906.

3. Manning to Mather, 4 January 1907.

4. The June 1906 issue of *Indoors and Out* featured an article by R. Clipston Strugis, "Of What Shall the House Be Built?" The article included three other projects by Platt. See Keith Morgan, "Gwinn: The Creation of the New American Landscape," in, *Shaping an American Landscape: The Art and Architecture of Charles A. Platt* (Hanover, N.H.: Hood Museum of Art/University Press of New England, forthcoming). I am grateful to Keith Morgan for making his book available to me in manuscript.

5. Manning to Mather, 11 February 1907.

6. Hutcheson to Mather, 23 February 1907.

7. Smyth to Mather, 12 March 1907. Collection of the Western Reserve Historical Society, Cleveland, container 23.

8. According to a letter to Mather's secretary, C. G. Heer, dated 1 March 1907, Platt could be reached in Detroit care of Russell Alger.

9. Mather to Platt, 1 March 1907.

10. Lay, "Interview with Platt," 127.

11. Platt to Mather, 11 March 1907.

12. Mather to Platt, 22 March 1907.

13. Mather to Platt, 27 April 1907.

14. Platt to Mather, 1 May 1907.

15. Mather to Platt, 5 May 1907.

16. Morgan, *Platt*, offers a broad assessment of Platt's country houses.

17. Platt to Mather, 27 April 1907.

18. Warren Manning, "Gwinn," unpublished manuscript, long version, undated, 5, WGM.

19. Ibid.

20. By 1907 Samuel had also decided to build a new house; he chose a lot back on Euclid Avenue, the same neighborhood William had just left. Samuel then had two houses, one in town and Shoreby (built in 1890), both of which had been designed by the Cleveland architect Charles Schweinfurth.

21. Mather to Manning, 28 May 1907.

22. Manning to Mather, 10 June 1907.

CHAPTER SIX

1. A founding member of the Garden Club of Cleveland in 1912, Kate Mather had a lively interest in horticulture. The new garden club's regulations limited membership to "those who are fortunate possessors of gardens of unusual perfection, and those who plan and develop personally and enthusiastically gardens of their own design." Gwinn probably qualified Kate under the first proviso, but she may also have been "personally and enthusiastically" helping develop the gardens at Gwinn. Sadly, time has obscured her role with regard to both the architecture and the landscape.

2. See Morgan, *Platt*, 118.

3. Platt to Mather, 27 June 1907.

4. Mather to Platt, 11 June 1907.

5. Platt to Mather, 13 July 1907.

6. Mather to Platt, 15 July 1907.

7. Platt to Mather, 16 July 1907.

8. Morgan, "Gwinn," n. 27.

9. Mather to Platt, 5 January 1908.

10. Mather to Platt, 25 March 1908.

11. The total cost of these items, not including Platt's 10-percent commission, was $30,814.99. This was only the first of many such trips.

12. Platt to Mather, 12 May 1908.

13. Platt to Mather, 11 April 1911.

CHAPTER SEVEN

1. Platt, *Italian Gardens*, 116.

2. Manning, "Gwinn," 4.

3. Mather to Manning, 8 September 1908; Mather to Platt, 8 September 1908.

4. Manning to Mather, 9 September 1908.

5. Ibid.

6. Manning to Mather, 3 October 1908. Information and quotations about plant selections in the following paragraphs are from this letter.

7. Cynthia Zaitzevsky, "Paul R. Frost of Cambridge: An Introduction to His Life and Work," *Journal of the New England Garden History Society* 2 (Fall 1992): 10–19. According to Zaitzevsky, Frost also worked on the Slade, McCormick, and Maxwell estates, all of which were designed by Platt.

8. Mather to Platt, 15 July 1908.

9. Ibid.

10. Platt to Mather, 16 July 1908; Mather to Platt, 20 October 1908.

11. Platt to Mather, 27 October 1908.

12. Manning to Mather, 9 September 1908.

13. Manning to Mather, 3 October 1908.

14. Manning to Mather, 4 November 1908.

15. Ibid.

16. Mather to Manning, 22 September 1910.

17. Manning to Mather, 13 October 1910.

18. Manning to Mather, 9 November 1908. Taylor's contributions to the profession were far-reaching. He served three terms as president of ASLA, was a contributing editor to *Landscape Architecture*, and wrote a book in 1929, *The Complete Garden*.

19. WMA, 265.

CHAPTER EIGHT

1. Mather to Platt, 7 September 1909.

2. Manning to Mather, 28 April 1909.

3. Mather to Manning, 21 June 1909.

4. Mather to Jacques, 3 September 1909.

5. Warren Manning, "Planting Notes and Report of Visit to Estate of Mr. William G. Mather," 16 September 1909, WGM.

6. Ibid.

7. Warren H. Manning, "Park Design and Planting" (speech to the Park and Outdoor Association, Louisville, Ky., 22 April 1897), MCL.

8. Manning to Mather, 30 September 1909.

9. Mather to Manning, 15 September 1910.

10. Mather to Platt, 5 August 1909.

11. Unidentified news article in scrapbook, WGM.

12. Mather to Manning, 16 April 1914; Manning to Mather, 18 April 1914.

CHAPTER NINE

1. Manning needed a rest. In 1909 his office took on 53 new jobs: a city parks plan for Scranton, Pa., a country club in Rio Vista, Va., a plan for Proximity Mills Manufacturing Company in Greensboro, N.C., the Bangor, Me., Public Library, and the Mount Tom Golf Club in Holyoke, Mass., were among them, along with several estates, schools, waterworks, cemetery plots, and three projects for the Cleveland-Cliffs Iron Ore Company in northern Michigan.

2. Mather to Manning, 15 September 1910.

3. Manning to Mather, 13 October 1910.

4. Mather to Platt, 22 September 1910.

5. Platt, *Italian Gardens*, 90.

6. Mather to Platt, 11 April 1911.

7. Manning to Mather, 13 November 1911.

8. During the same years that Manning was struggling with Gwinn's wild garden, he was developing an ambitious landscape plan for Frank and Gertrude Seiberling, in nearby Akron. Unlike Gwinn, however, Stan Hywet's wild garden formed the heart of the design. Manning's role in the Akron project differed substantially from the one he played at Gwinn. At Stan Hywet, Manning was designated principal landscape architect. As such he advised in the selection of property, sited the house, determined the overall landscape plan, collaborated on the design of all terraces, porches, and other architectural extensions from the house, and determined planting designs. In his collaboration with the Seiberlings' architect, Charles Schneider, Manning had a dominant role. As a result, several of the major features at Stan Hywet—the birch allée, the London plane tree allée, the great lawn, and especially the wild garden—were determined by plantings and natural features, not by architecture. The scale of Stan Hywet proved more accommodating to Manning's approach than had the home grounds of Gwinn.

9. Mather to Platt, 17 November 1914.

10. Platt to Mather, 19 November 1914 and 22 April 1915.

CHAPTER TEN

1. The costs of Gwinn's fountains and sculpture were recorded as follows: wall fountain (north terrace)—$1,600; lion/sphinxes—$1,750; terrace fountain (not including bronze figure)—$1,350; formal garden fountain (not including bronze figure)—$3,520; marble planter at turn of drive—$2,250; dolphin fountain (wild garden)—$8,080 (memorandum, 7 March 1911).

2. Mather to Platt, 24 June 1916.

3. Mather to Platt, 8 May 1912 and 15 May 1914.

4. Morgan, *Platt*, 201.

5. Platt to Mather, 26 August 1912.

6. Platt to Mather, 10 October 1912.

7. Mather to Platt, 15 October 1912; Platt to Mather, 15 October 1912.

CHAPTER ELEVEN

1. Mather to Manning, 18 December 1912; WMA, 32.

2. Manning, "Gwinn" (short version), 32–33. The shorter version appears to have been the result of editing, as its language is more formal. See Appendix II for a plant list for the wild garden, compiled from Manning's notes.

3. Manning to E. E. Boalt, 5 February 1913.

4. Four of the bridges were constructed in 1921 from chestnuts killed by the chestnut blight; they came from the Manning manse in Billerica, Mass.

5. Platt to Mather, 24 January 1913.

6. Manning to Heer, 5 February 1913.

7. Manning to Jacques, 5 February 1913.

8. Ibid.

9. Manning to Heer, 19 February 1913.

10. Manning to Mather, 13 May 1913. Manning's approach to wild gardens is chronicled in many of his writings but perhaps nowhere so clearly as in an undated (certainly early) essay, "The Nature Garden" (MCL). In this short article Manning offers the view that the wild garden is already a part of nature and the designer's job is to reveal it through judicious thinning, pruning, and grubbing out. Manning goes on to advocate for the inclusion of an unusually broad plant palette, including "trees, shrubs, herbs, mosses, lichens, fungi, and algae all of which may be incidents well worth ... developing when their beauty is fully recognized" (1). Manning's highly original approach reflects the influence of both his Emersonian roots and his Yankee practicality.

11. WMA, 295.

12. WMA, 250–51.

13. Manning to Mather, 25 May 1915. Manning's fee for "general oversight" at Gwinn, once most the major developments were completed, was $300 for four visits per year, "plus the necessary office, drafting and clerical expenses and a proportionate share of the travelling expenses." Manning to Mather, 5 May 1914.

14. Mather to Platt, 23 October 1913.

15. Mather to Platt, 29 October 1913.

16. Platt to Mather, 28 October 1913.

17. Betty Gabrielli, "The Oral History of Paul R. Young: Horticulturist, Educator, Writer, Husband, Father," based on interviews, 10 August–21 September 1986, 24, WGM. Young also worked closely with Elizabeth Mather in the country relief gardens program, which she directed as chairperson.

18. Cornelia Ireland to author, undated.

CHAPTER TWELVE

1. Mather to Platt, 15 January 1914; Platt to Mather, 7 February 1914.

2. "Memorandum of Directions, Etc., Given by Mrs. Shipman at Gwinn, April 9th, in Consultation with Miss Mather, Mr. Wm. G. Mather and George Jacques," 9 April 1914, WGM.

3. Shipman to Mather, 24 April 1914.

4. Ibid.

5. Mather to Shipman, 12 June 1914.

6. Unidentified newspaper article in scrapbook, WGM.

7. "Woman Manages 55-Acre Estate of W. G. Mather," 2 September 1927, and "Plants—and Dogs—Grow for Her," 11 February 1927, unidentified news clippings in scrapbook marked "Gwinn," WGM.

8. The *William G. Mather* is now open to the public as a museum operated by the Great Lakes Historical Society and anchored at the East 9th Street Pier in Cleveland. For more information, see the society's quarterly journal, *Inland Seas*, June 1990.

9. Mather to Platt, 10 October 1927.

10. William Mathewson Milliken, *A Time Remembered: A Cleveland Memoir* (Cleveland: Western Reserve Historical Society, 1975), 140.

11. Mather to Platt, 15 July 1929. The first painters considered for the job were Rockwell Kent and, at William Platt's suggestion, Barry Faulkner, but neither was available. Platt then recommended George de Forest Brush (whom he knew from Cornish), who made two models for the scheme in November 1929. "The plan of lighting and detail," wrote Platt, "is to be mod-

ern in every way.... His scheme is exceedingly interesting. Parts of it, however, are so far from the standards to which we are accustomed that it cannot be criticised from that point of view! Personally I would like to see the thing put through," (Platt to Mather, 27 November 1929).

12. Mather to Platt, 8 November 1929.

13. Ibid. and 23 November 1929.

14. Mather to Platt, 23 November 1929.

15. If Elizabeth Mather's creativity did not find unlimited range in new, permanent decorating schemes for the house, it was clearly evident in her temporary decorations for social and family events at Gwinn. One party in 1956 surpassed all previous efforts. In Gwinn's living room Elizabeth re-created the scene of two of her friends' betrothal many years earlier, a cottage porch swing at a Michigan summer camp on Higgins Lake. To evoke the lakeside landscape, Elizabeth removed all the furniture from her living room and ordered three tons of sand dumped on the floor. Michigan pine trees were imported for the "woods." Hidden lights and screens were arranged to simulate the flicker of lights on the lake's surface. A porch swing was hung from a mock porch. The guests, needless to say, were dazzled. After the party, Elizabeth had the sand shoveled into Gwinn's basement, formerly William's billiard room. There she created a tropical paradise for her grandchildren, complete with ocean mural and life-size papier-mâché palm trees.

CHAPTER THIRTEEN

1. Manning to Mather, 15 November 1933 and 22 January 1935.

2. Manning to Mather, 30 September 1930. Cyrus McCormick sent Mather a note—"I am doing the same interesting work that you are"—along with a copy of *Landscape Art*, 24 November 1930.

3. Several versions of this still–unpublished autobiography are in MCL.

4. Manning to Mather, 16 November 1930. Both versions are in WGM.

5. Mather to Manning, 9 February 1931.

6. Mather to Manning, 6 December 1932.

7. Manning to Mather, 25 July 1934.

8. Mather to Manning, 6 August 1934. Mather's letter also described a recent visit from Mrs. Francis (Louisa) King, a well-known garden writer and designer who was in town to address the garden club: "She spoke very highly of you, your character and attainments; and she also was feeling very hard up and disturbed on account of the lack of [work]."

9. Manning to Mather, 8 September 1934.

10. Mather to Manning, 8 May 1933; Mather to Platt, 24 May 1933.

11. Mather to Manning, 8 May 1933.

12. Manning to Mather, 22 May 1933.

CHAPTER FOURTEEN

1. Ellen Shipman's fee for the new planting plans was $200.

2. Mather to Shipman, 30 September 1935.

3. Ibid.

4. Ibid.

5. Since Shipman left no notes concerning future maintenance for this area, questions remain about her intentions. Certainly she realized that tree lilacs grow to great size and would eventu-

ally crowd out the small trees. Whether she envisioned intense pruning or ongoing replacement so that sizes could be kept small is not known.

6. See Appendix III for a complete plant list.

7. Mather to Manning, 21 March 1936.

8. Mather to Manning, 25 February 1936. Manning's fee for the supervisory work was $50 per day, plus expenses. Manning to Mather, 27 February 1936.

9. Manning and Webb to Mather, 17 March 1936.

10. Mather to Manning, 26 May 1936; Manning to Mather, 5 June 1936.

11. Mather to Manning, 2 June 1937. These letters, curiously, are not among those in the archives.

12. Manning to Mather, 22 December 1935.

13. Cornelia Ireland to author, undated.

EPILOGUE

1. In 1930 Doris Humphrey and Charles Weidman performed at Gwinn; nine years later, Agnes De Mille danced there, accompanied by members of the Cleveland Symphony.

2. Milliken, *Time Remembered*, 183–84.

INDEX

Page numbers in italics refer to illustrations.

Parrish, Maxfield (painter), 15, 16, 17, 18
Parsons Jr., Samuel (landscape architect), 28
"Perils of Society" (film), 138
Piccirilli Studio, New York (sculptors), 101, 107, 111. *See also* Gwinn estate: sculpture
Pickands, Mather and Company, 37. *See also* Cleveland–Cliffs Iron Company
Pinchot, Gifford. *See* Biltmore
Platt, Charles Adams, *14, 39*
    biographical information: art training (New York), 15–16; childhood, 15; death, 154; death of brother, 18; death of first wife, 16; in Cornish, 16–17; in Italy, 16, 17, 18; in *Landscape Architecture,* 20–21; monograph on, 4, 147; in Paris, 15–16
    career, 20–21; choice as architect at Gwinn, 46–48; effect of Depression on, 154; effect of WWI on, 137–38
    critiques of his work, 18–19, 47
    design approach: interior, 61; landscape, 11, 18–21; as complementary to Manning's, 23
    personality, 20
    professional relationships: with landscape architects, 189–90n16; with Mather, 59; role at Gwinn, 86; with Shipman, 31–32
    projects: Croly residence (Cornish, N.H.), 30; Deerfield Academy (Deerfield, Mass.), 154; Faulkner Farm (Brookline, Mass.), 18, 47; Hanna Building Cleveland, Ohio), 39; Ireland family home (Saginaw, Mich.), 140, 145; Leader Building (Cleveland, Ohio), 39; Phillips Academy (Andover, Mass.), 154; Platt residence (Cornish, N.H.), 17, 18, 31; University of Illinois (Urbana), 154; Weld (Brookline, Mass.), 47
    writings: *Harper's Magazine* article, 18; *Italian Gardens,* 18
Platt, Geoffrey (Charles's son), 111, 154
Platt, William (Charles's brother), 18, 23, 197n.11
Platt, William (Charles's son), 154
Platt, Wyckoff and Coles (architects), 173
Poins House (Plainfield, N.H.), 30–31. *See also* Shipman, Ellen Biddle
Pope, Theodate (Manning client), 26–27
Pratt, Nellie Hamblin (Manning's wife), 23

residential design, 13, 19. *See also* American Country House movement
Robinson, William (landscape designer), 8, 187n1. *See also* formal/informal style debate

Rockefeller Sr., John D. (Cleveland resident), 36, 39

Saginaw, Mich. *See* Platt, Charles Adams: projects
Saint-Gaudens, Augustus, 16, 17, 30, 113
Sarah Duke Memorial Garden (Durham, N.C.), 33. *See also* Shipman, Ellen Biddle
Sargent, Charles Sprague (Brookline, Mass.), garden of, 70
Schmidt, Mott B. (architect), 32. *See also* Shipman, Ellen Biddle
Schneider, Charles (architect), 7, 195n8. *See also* Stan Hywet Hall
Seiberling, Frank (Manning client), 27, 150, 195n8
Severence, John L. (Cleveland resident), 38
Shinn, Everett (Cornish artist), 16
Shipman, Ellen Biddle, *29*
    approach to landscape design, 32–33
    biographical information: childhood, 29–30; in Cornish, 16, 17, 30; death, 29; development of interest in landscape architecture, 29, 30; education, 30; encouragement by Platt, 31; marriage, 30
    career, 32–33; at Gwinn, 135–37, 157–58, 162–63; New York office, 33
    House and Garden on, 31, 33
    influence of Gertrude Jekyll on, 33
    landscape legacy, 33
    Manning's opinion of, 28
    professional relationships: with architects, 32; collaboration with Platt, 31–32; conflict with Jacques, 84, 136–37
    projects: Willard Clapp, 39; in Cleveland, 39; Halfred Farms (Chagrin Falls, Ohio), 39; Lake Shore Boulevard (Grosse Pointe Shores, Mich.), 33; Longue Vue (New Orleans, La.), 33; Mercantile Building (New York), 190n18; nonresidential, 33; Sarah Duke Memorial Garden (Durham, N.C.), 3; Shipman residences (Brook Place, Cornish, and Poins House, Plainfield, N.H.), 30–31; Edgar Stern, 33; Windsor White, 39
    on women in the profession, 32
Shipman, Louis (Ellen's husband), 17, 30–31
Shoreby (S. Mather, Cleveland, Ohio), 43
Shurcliff, Arthur (landscape architect), 30
Smith, General Jared A., 56. *See also* Gwinn estate: architectural features (seawall)
Stan Hywet Hall (Seiberling, Akron, Ohio): and